THE LEFT BOOK CLUB

Victor Gollancz at a Trafalgar Square Rally during the period
of the Left Book Club

THE LEFT BOOK CLUB

AN HISTORICAL RECORD

by

JOHN LEWIS

With a Foreword by
Dame Margaret Cole

LONDON
VICTOR GOLLANCZ LTD
1970

Z
549
.L4L45

ACKNOWLEDGEMENTS

I am most grateful to the many former members of the Left
Book Club who sent in documents, minutes of Group meetings
and personal reminiscences; to Mrs Olga Miller for permission
to print a poem by Sagittarius which first appeared in the *New
Statesman*; and also to Stuart Samuels for his American research
essay on the Club, and Gordon Barrick Neavill for his Dissert-
ation on the Left Book Club to the Faculty of the Graduate
Library School, Chicago—a thorough and illuminating piece
of work from an outside point of view that proved most helpful.

J.L.

MADE AND PRINTED IN GREAT BRITAIN BY
THE GARDEN CITY PRESS LIMITED
LETCHWORTH, HERTFORDSHIRE

CONTENTS

FOREWORD

VICTOR GOLLANCZ'S Left Book Club, of which John Lewis here tells the detailed story, was founded in May of 1936. Its peak, when it registered 57,000 members and 1,500 "Left Discussion Groups", was in 1939, at the outbreak of war.

These dates are important. It is often assumed, by people whose knowledge or recollection of the inter-war years is rather imprecise, that the Left Book Club came into existence as an immediate result of the economic crash of 1929–1932, of the fate of the second Labour Government, and of the state of misery, depression and repression which afflicted Britain immediately afterwards. This is not the case: the Left Book Club, as a matter of fact, came into being at a moment when hopes, albeit faint hopes, were beginning to oust the despair of the early thirties which was so well depicted in Walter Greenwood's best-seller, *Love on the Dole*. For these hopes there was more than one reason. *First*, the conditions of life for the working classes were undoubtedly improving: even if this improvement was far smaller than it ought to have been. It was at last achieved, it is salutary to remember, largely at the expense of the overseas producers of primary foods and materials whose price in the world market had fallen so catastrophically. Nevertheless the improvement was *there*, and it encouraged its recipients to ask for more, both for themselves and for those groups which had yet to feel the benefit, like the shipyard workers of Jarrow, the Town that was Murdered. *Second*, the intellectuals and the professionals had recovered sufficiently from the immediate impact of the world slump to think again and to reach the conclusion that neither world slumps nor the resultant miseries could be allowed to recur—and that intelligent organisation could prevent them. People were learning from Maynard Keynes about deficit spending and the management of money: doctors like John Boyd-Orr were telling them how scandalous, and how wasteful it was to expect the unemployed and their families to live on the sort of rations that State benefit would provide for them: "starving in the midst of plenty" was *not* a law of the universe. *Lastly*, signs appeared that the political scene, even, might be changing. Roosevelt's New Deal had many flaws, no doubt; but it was better than what had gone before. The British general election of 1935 showed some progress; and in France Leon Blum's *Front Populaire* was actually coming into being—and within a very few months, about to come into power. After the deadly years, what Henry Nevinson had called the Stage-Army of the Good was beginning to take heart for battle; and when a highly successful publisher appeared ready to put his money—and still more his organisation—into the forefront of that battle, the rank and file of that army rushed to enlist.

Some of the forty-four "first choices" of the Club—the books which, at the price of half-a-crown were provided monthly for every member—were therefore devoted to spelling out clearly the horrors which must be got rid of. But not very many, for most of the membership knew about the horrors already; what they wanted to be told was how to get rid of them, and this implied a change in the direction at the top. So that, in retrospect, and looking through the list of publications printed by Lewis at the end of his book, one sees that the bulk of the forty-four, as well as of the hundred others issued by the Club during this period of three and a half years, was aimed essentially at creating a Popular Front in Britain comparable with what Blum had created in France—and doing it through informed knowledge of what was happening in other countries as widely separated as Spain and China, and through knitting the members of the Club together by means of a growing number of ancillary enterprises like the *Left News*, the Discussion Groups, the rallies, week-ends and summer schools (all chronicled by Lewis), in the hope of converting a reading public into a real movement.

But the movement never came into being: and the list of books also shows the reason. For increasingly their titles give out warnings of what was likely to happen—of the menace which was building up fast in central Europe, where there was a live movement, but a movement which was horrible; but the books and the rallies and the summer schools failed to convince the British people, and particularly the British Labour Party, that the menace was really so serious. Their suspicions—their very justified suspicions, as documents produced in the Nuremberg Trials and elsewhere have abundantly proved—of the Tory leaders held them back; and when at last in the summer of Dunkirk a real Popular Front came into being, the Club, for a variety of reasons, had already passed its peak of influence. What it had effectively done was not apparent until five years later, when Left books like *Tory M.P.* and *Guilty Men* (both concerned as much with pre-war as with later conditions) played their large part in the 1945 election, and the British electorate showed quite clearly that they believed, as the founders of the Club had told them, that the conditions of the thirties must never never return.

Lewis's book is devoted to one organisation only: there were of course others existing and struggling at the same time for the same main purpose. But of these—of the Socialist League and the New Fabian Research Bureau, to take only two examples—the records are very scanty and full of gaps. The Left Book Club had the great advantage, for the student of the times, that its publisher-founder had a great enthusiasm both for it and for an organisation which could make and preserve records; so that in this book the student can find out just what it was and how it worked. Would that we had something similar for Robert Blatchford's Clarion Clubs, Clarion Scouts and Clarion Vanners in the days of the *Clarion's* glory seventy years ago. Meanwhile, let us be grateful for what we have.

MARGARET COLE

CHAPTER I

THE LAUNCHING OF THE CLUB

It is difficult to recall the years between the great depression of 1929 to 1931 and the formation of the Left Book Club in May, 1936. They were unhappy years which we would like to forget. They witnessed the aftermath of a catastrophic collapse of the whole economy of the Western world, with much continuing unemployment, the despairing poverty of the distressed areas, the painful and dishearteningly slow climb back to normality. They witnessed too the dramatic consequence of this crisis in Germany: the rise of Hitler and his "National Socialists", the Nazis.

Then came the Franco revolution in Spain: the military insurrection against the moderate coalition government of Liberals and Socialists resulting from the elections of February 1936. Finally there was the disheartening threefold failure of the League of Nations: to stop Japan's invasion of Manchuria; to stop Mussolini's invasion of Abyssinia; and very soon to confront, with paralysed will and utter impotence, the rise of Hitler, the invasion of the Rhineland, the absorption of Austria, the rape of Czechoslovakia.

The deep anxiety, the feeling of apprehension during those years can hardly be imagined by those who did not live through them. No-one has expressed the bitterness of that time more eloquently than Lady Violet Bonham Carter (later Baroness Asquith).

Tranquillity, Safety First, Appeasement—these were the watchwords behind which the British people marched, or rather crawled, throughout the thirties.

Translated into practice, Tranquillity meant the passive acceptance of great social ills such as mass unemployment in our midst; Safety First was the policy which led us so blindly and unprepared into the Second World War; Appeasement was the pursuit of peace at any price which other people could be made to pay.[1]

Confronted with these perils and disasters neither Conservative, nor Labour, nor Liberal had anything to offer—no constructive policies were put forward to deal with unemployment, apart from restrictions on spending. It was considered enough to leave things to the operation of economic laws to work themselves out. Many in high places were sympathetic to fascism, which they saw as the only alternative to socialism. Their policies were reinforced by the moral cowardice and wishful thinking of too many of the political leaders and advisers of the government.

It was in these circumstances that there began simultaneously, and in many different directions, an awakening of public concern and a new endeavour for understanding. This did not always appear among the regular members and supporters of the political parties, but to a considerable extent among the non-politicals, the intellectuals and the professional classes, and also among those hardest hit by the depression. This concern ranged from members of the universities to the miners and the organised unemployed, from social workers and parsons to city clerks and research scientists.

Playing its own special role in this awakening was the *Left Book Club* with rapidly growing numbers that reached some 57,000 by the war years, and with 1,500 organised study groups. Its aim was "to help in the terribly urgent struggle for World Peace and against Fascism by giving to all who are determined to play their part in this struggle such knowledge as will immensely increase their efficiency."

It was a response to the growing menace of Hitler's policies and German rearmament. All sections of Left opinion were represented in the movement, which was determined not to follow the fateful example of Germany, which in 1933 was overrun by the Nazis because the opponents of Hitler failed to unite in common defence, and for that reason, divided, fell easy victims to the Nazi seizure of power. It saw the hope for world peace only in a policy of collective security, including both France *and Russia,* realising that without the help of Russia,

[1] E. Spier, *Focus, A History of The Thirties* (Wolff, 1963) from the *Introduction* by Lady Violet Bonham Carter.

whatever the risks involved, there was not the slightest hope of holding Hitler in check.

We all remember those of the Left who took this position : but we are not so familiar with such names as Dr Edith Summerskill, M.P., Sir Walter Layton, Sir Norman Angell, Lord Addison, Sir Peter Chalmers Mitchell, and Eleanor Rathbone, who gave their whole-hearted support to the cause of collective security, and all appeared on the platform of the Left Book Club.

The *political* moves to bring into existence what came to be called a "Popular Front" were, however, never the responsibility of the Club. Its self-imposed task was to create the clear understanding out of which alone effective measures such as the formation of the Popular Front could come. Most of the members, indeed, believed that such measures would ultimately involve the unity of people of all parties of the Left. The meetings organised by the Club on specific issues did in fact bring together leading personalities of all such parties and of none. But they were always concerned with the questions in hand. The Club never moved to create a union of parties or a new *ad hoc* party embracing representatives of all the parties. Its sole object was to enlighten, to educate.

The aim of the Club, like that of the men of the Enlightenment in the age of Reason, who created the movement of political reform which culminated in the American War of Independence of 1776 and the French Revolution of 1789, was "by speech and pen to make men more enlightened." The Left Book Club, undeterred by those who were coming to believe that reason was powerless, returned to the principles of "enlightenment" as the ultimate defence of democracy and popular rights, in the belief that there can be no effective democratic government where the people are not informed, and where rational discussion does not sift truth from error.

It therefore became the function of the Left Book Club to supply relevant information and theoretical analysis of the problems of the day, whether an inquiry into the rise of Hitler or Mussolini, or the story of Mao Tse Tung's great march in China; whether a detailed study of unemployment, or a medical report on the extent and consequences to health of poverty in the distressed areas.

The purpose of the Club was to produce a series of books

dealing with the three closely related questions of fascism, the threat of war, and poverty, aiming at effective resistance to the first, the prevention of the second, and socialism as a cure for the third. Launched by the publisher Victor Gollancz, the books were to be selected by him, John Strachey and Harold Laski, and published monthly at the lowest possible price.

The first advertisement for the Club appeared in March 1936, and in May the first book was published: *France Today and the People's Front* by Maurice Thorez. It was hoped, with luck, to have 2,500 members by then. Instead the first book was subscribed by 5,000 members, and the membership rapidly rose to 20,000 as the year ended.

It was, however, not the aim of the Club to publish only books of a political nature. The intention was to produce and circulate books of a wide range—sociological, philosophical and biographical—not directly connected with the events of the day, but providing that background of knowledge and understanding without which we may have politics, but not enlightenment.

In London and the larger cities the Club grew rapidly, and it also found members in the industrial North and in South Wales. The universities at once responded and before long there were some 300 members in Cambridge alone. From the very first, a News Sheet of announcements was issued with each book. This was initially called the *Left Book News*. It contained notices and reviews of forthcoming books, articles on the "Topic of the Month" and, for instance, regular articles on Soviet Russia.

The first number appeared in May. In the June number a short list of local study circles was given as a result of the suggestion by several readers that they should meet "to discuss the issues raised by the monthly Choice." The names of five persons appeared, and readers living in the same locality were invited to get in touch with them. The first of these names was that of Joseph Gordon Macleod, The Manor House, Hemingford Grey, Huntingdonshire.

Joseph Macleod, actor and poet, thus became the first convener of a Left Book Club Group. In the July issue there were twenty-three further names; and the first was that of Frank Allaun, now (1970) Labour Member of Parliament for East Salford. The groups increased rapidly and by the end of 1936 they were being formed at the rate of fifty a month.

It was clear that this represented an upsurge of passionate

interest, and a desire to find out what was happening in the world of 1936 and what to do about it.

As Strachey said at the first Albert Hall Rally in February 1937:

"How can it have happened? The answer is, of course, that it could only have happened at the present moment, in the present situation in the world. It is only today, when we are facing a situation incomparably graver, incomparably more dangerous than any which we have known before, that an organisation of this sort, devoted to the equipment of its members to meet this situation could have grown at this extraordinary speed."

The times called urgently for the kind of enlightenment that only the wide dissemination of literature could provide. But until the situation was met by an individual aware of the need and competent to fulfil it, no such thing was likely to happen. There would have been no Left Book Club but for Victor Gollancz, or someone with his qualities, and the backing of an established publishing house.

We know of the immediate occasion of the Club's formation. John Strachey, at the first Albert Hall Rally of the Club on February 7th, 1937, told the audience of a private meeting at a Soho restaurant called by Sir Stafford Cripps to consider the founding of a socialist weekly. This was early in 1936. As they were leaving Gollancz said to him, "Do you know, I believe that the next thing is some sort of Left Book Club; will you help me to select the books?" Strachey agreed and they decided to ask Laski to join them. Gollancz continues the story. "I rang Laski up before breakfast the next morning, and he also immediately agreed. So the Left Book Club was founded".[2]

Undoubtedly the key figure was Victor Gollancz with his financial resources and publishing firm. He was however a great deal more than a successful publisher. From his Oxford days he had been a socialist, and as a schoolmaster he had realised the importance of political education and debate.

He was at New College, Oxford, in the years preceding the First World War. Although, due to the war, he left Oxford prematurely, without taking a degree, he took the preliminary

[2] *Left News* (August 1945).

examination to Greats—Classical Moderations—in the language and literature of Greece and Rome "and got a first—indeed, a good first, a specially good one"[3], and won the Chancellor's Prize for Latin Prose for "A Dialogue on Socialism".[4]

The outbreak of war in 1914 brought his university career to an end. He was called up at first, but was soon "directed to other employment." Arriving at Repton, the Headmaster of which was Fisher, subsequently to become the Archbishop of Canterbury,[5] he not only became a highly successful teacher of classics for university scholarships, but, deeply concerned as he was at the international situation and the tragedy of the war, he was appalled at the ignorance and apathy of masters and boys to political affairs. Along with David Somervell, later to emerge as a distinguished historian, he did in 1916 very much what he was to do again on a much larger scale twenty years later. He organised a voluntary discussion forum on current affairs, which shook the conventional institution of Repton to its foundations. He and Somervell went further and issued a periodical, "a serious journal on the lines of the *Spectator* or *Nation,* to canalise the political waters that were swirling into spate." It was called *A Public School Looks at the World,* and it created something of a sensation in London, and even appeared in a well known socialist bookshop in Charing Cross Road.[6]

The boys responded with enthusiasm. They found a new interest in life. They started reading widely. Gollancz insisted on every side of these controversial issues being fairly and fully stated, even though he never concealed his socialist convictions. The experiment came to an abrupt conclusion. The War Office intervened. Gollancz was asked to resign, the paper and the discussions came to an end.

In collaboration with David Somervell, his colleague on the staff at Repton, Gollancz published *Political Education at a Public School* (Collins, 1918), and later he wrote *The School and the World* (Chapman and Hall, 1918). Both books have within

---

[3] *My Dear Timothy,* p. 221, Victor Gollancz Ltd, 1952. *More for Timothy,* p. 156, Victor Gollancz Ltd, 1953.
[4] There is a copy in the British Museum Library, and it is very well worth reading.
[5] The Rev. Geoffrey Fisher, now Lord Fisher of Lambeth.
[6] Now Collet's Bookshop.

them the principles and aims of political education, which he afterwards worked out in the Left Book Club.

Gollancz carried away from Repton a burning conviction that political education is important : "not merely desirable but a matter of life or death." He believed that, "as an instrument for education the discipline of politics is a discipline like no other." What is the world crying out for?

> Good men of course : but men capable of applying their goodness in the national no less than in the personal sphere, and in the international no less than in the national. And this can be done in one way only—on the basis of knowledge : knowledge of facts; knowledge of ideas; knowledge of the motives that have moved human beings and still continue to move them, often so obscurely. Without it a man is at the mercy of any unscrupulous demagogue or shrieking newspaper, and we plunge on with increasing precipitancy from one disaster to another.[7]

Of the first importance was the way Gollancz dealt with the question of propaganda. How far is it proper in education? This was to be a crucial question for the Club, and one which increasingly troubled his conscience. He was sure that the presentation of any vital issue in a perfectly balanced and passionless manner would only result in boredom and loss of moral earnestness. He decided that any writer or teacher or speaker must present his own point of view openly and with all the enthusiasm he feels for it; but he should make it plain that it is *his* view, and cannot be accepted on his authority. On the contrary it must be examined critically. Therefore the opposing view must be stated either by himself, with the genuine endeavour to put that case as strongly as he can, or by someone else. But regarding the presentation of one's own view, "I call this a sort of propaganda, because a glow, a sense of dreadfully caring, is imparted to the presentation that cannot be imparted to the opposing view, by the supporter of the first, however honestly he tries to do so."[8] To state one's own deeply felt convictions and also the opposing view, V.G. felt to be difficult but not impossible.

The problem arose acutely in connection with the Club and

[7] *More for Timothy.*
[8] *More for Timothy*, p. 316.

its opposition to fascism, and he was aware of it. Was he then willing for "the other side" to have an equal opportunity for presentation? Of course he did not think so. And most people would agree. Nevertheless it worried him profoundly that he had to be one-sided when the fascist threat confronted Western civilization. That earnest desire for balance rather than partiality was to emerge again in his thoughts during the period following the 1938 Munich Agreement.

In 1920, after Repton and his war service, Gollancz edited a series of small volumes (published by Humphrey Milford) dealing with current issues, under the general title, "The World of Today", one of which, *Industrial Ideals,* he wrote himself. This little book tells us a lot about its author. The utopian socialist of New College was still a socialist: "Socialism," he wrote, "is a question which is held to be of more importance than any other contemporary issue." He proceeds to state with all possible fairness the case for State Socialism, for Syndicalism, for Guild Socialism, and for the Soviet System. He then proceeds to balance this exposition from the standpoint of liberal reform and individualism; attempting, as he did at Repton, to state with scrupulous impartiality all that could be said on all sides. Thus the individualist critic replies to the socialist:

> Have you not been carried so away by impatience and indignation that you have forgotten to respect the thought and conscience not only of what you call the exploiting class, but even of the mass of workers themselves?

Nevertheless it is apparent that his sympathies are with socialism, and emphatically with the Guild Socialism then being expounded by G. D. H. Cole and S. G. Hobson. Hence the emphasis is on the control of each industry by the workers in it (workers by hand and brain), economic control of the national economy being in the hands of an economic council of all the industrial unions concerned. In his work at Repton, and in this series of volumes, we can see him grappling, to use his own words at the time, with "the great ideas, the great movements, which are battling for mastery in the world today."

Gollancz now turned to what was to be his life work—publishing. In 1921 he entered the firm of Ernest Benn Ltd, and in 1927 he was issuing a series of paper-covered books by first-rate authorities on a wide range of topics. They were "Benn's Sixpenny Library"—really a precursor of the *Pelicans* of later years. About 250 of these little books appeared and they were well selected and admirably written.

But he was very soon to set up as a publisher on his own account. The new firm quickly became known both for its books and their typography—especially for their book jackets in bold types, black and magenta, on yellow paper. As Gollancz said,

> It is the proper business of effective business printing to include provocation among its consistent virtues . . . to be effective, you must surprise—startle.[9]

Part of Gollancz's list consisted of popular fiction and detective stories, but whatever he was publishing there was no doubt about "his almost uncanny gift for gauging the possibilities of any book offered to him."[10] The choice, the typography and striking appearance, were followed by spectacular advertising, the copy for which he wrote himself. Finally he added to his list the informative books on politics and economics which he began to publish—at exceptionally low prices for books running to five or six hundred pages—in very large editions. For instance, *The Outline of Modern Knowledge,* by a remarkable team of writers, consisted of over 1,000 pages and sold more than 75,000 copies, first at eight shillings and sixpence, and then at six shillings.

It would be a mistake to forget the general list, but what claimed most attention in the thirties were the political books which were published to meet the urgent problems of the economic crisis and the political upheavals in Europe. Here lay his real mission, and the fulfilment of the ambitions of those early years at Repton and after. "Hatred of war came rushing up again in me," he wrote, "with a force of something newly awakened . . . So I asked myself, what little could *I* do?—and answered 'you can help to enlighten people, you can show them that, if capitalism persists, this sort of crisis is inevitable, and the final result will be war'—that was the beginning of my active political publishing."[11]

---

[9] John Carter, *Books and Book Collecting,* World Publishing Coy (New York), 1957.
[10] *Ibid.*
[11] *More for Timothy.*

Among these first publications in the crisis years were G. D. H. Cole's *Intelligent Man's Guide Through World Chaos* (1932), R. P. Dutt's *World Politics 1918–1936* (1936), Strachey's *Coming Struggle for Power* (1933), and many other such volumes. But as the thirties drew on the business of enlightening people took second place to the need for preventing a war that was just around the corner—and not only war, but the fascist threat to every form of progress, political and social. "Our very salvation," Gollancz believed, "depends on the political education of the masses."

Gollancz saw the urgent need of clear thinking, of scientific economic analysis, of radical political thinking. Once again it was "political education" that was demanded. In his auto-biographical volume, *More for Timothy,* he tells us what was behind the publication of these books.

That was the beginning of my active political publishing . . . It was political publishing that I thought about night and day . . . The passion to make people *see* that what had come blazing up thirty years before was again in my vitals; and now, I thought I would really do something about it. So I got going; I began pouring out a great mass of informative books, all with the familiar yellow covers. The most important of them, at this time, was G. D. H. Cole's *Intelligent Man's Guide Through World Chaos* : a vast tome, full of facts and figures, which I issued in an enormous edition at a ludicrously low price.

It had always been difficult to find a publisher for radical books, and this was not because they were badly written. Nor were the bookshops at all helpful in stocking them if they were published. "Such books," says Gollancz, "were rare exceptions, and ninety-nine booksellers out of a hundred quietly boycotted socialism."[12] One of his travellers, disappointed at a poor sub-scription for a new book on economic questions, asked the bookseller why. He replied that if the book had been written from a conservative standpoint he would have ordered ten times as many. This conspiracy of silence among the communicators, not only publishers and booksellers, grew in effectiveness rather than diminished as the perils of the time became more threaten-ing. It was not of course a deliberate policy, but more an

[12] *Left News* (August 1945).

instinctive reluctance to consider any fundamental contradiction of or challenge to the accepted way of viewing things.

Victor Gollancz as a publisher now became widely known and enthusiastically welcomed in progressive circles and by the new and growing reading public—alert, intelligent and appreciative, ready to buy and read serious left-wing books to an extent previously undreamt of by either publishers or booksellers.

It was clear that there was a public ready to buy the books, and that the books needed would be forthcoming once publication was possible. The stage was set for the launching of the Club.

There had been two main obstacles to the wide reading of the kind of books that so many people wanted to be made available: first the high prices of such books, and secondly, from the publisher's point of view, the difficulty of being sure of a market. Closely connected with the difficulty of selling such books was the fact that they were unlikely to be reviewed or to appear in the bookshops. Gollancz saw a way out if he could get a large number of people to *undertake* to buy books provided they were published at a sufficiently low price.

The Club was launched on the basis of a selected "Book of the Month" at half-a-crown. Each book was new—never before published, and was simultaneously published in hard covers at four or five times the price.

CHAPTER II

BUILDING THE CLUB

THE CLUB HAD not only to be launched, it had to be built and organised, and above all it had to grow. The first job was the books—the monthly choice; and after finding the initial books to distribute, there was the commissioning of further books to be written. This was immensely difficult; few people can produce a first-class book in a year, and to time. John Strachey could and did; the succession of books from his pen could be relied upon and they were eagerly read.

The selectors were V.G., as Victor Gollancz came to be called, Strachey and Harold Laski. Laski brought the authority of his academic prestige to the club, and he was always informed of what was going on, and occasionally consulted; but, though his support and loyalty were never in question, he did not in fact play a significant part in the development of the Club. Strachey worked consistently and indefatigably with V.G., discussing every book and every new development. He was the constructive thinker, with a first-rate knowledge of economic and political theory which Gollancz did not possess.

Next came recruiting. This depended on the advertising genius of V.G., his skill in choice of type, layout, crisp clear wording, and intelligibility. Thus there arrived the famous yellow leaflet :

PLEASE use this leaflet to get a new member.

These went out with every book, and the blank form on the back was to be filled in and despatched to the publishing office in Henrietta Street, where they arrived in ever increasing numbers.

On June 24th, in the second number of *The Left Book News*, V.G. wrote, "By the first post on Monday of this week we received close on six hundred applications for membership." In

March 1937 the membership had reached 39,400. By this time Left Book Club lectures and public meetings were being organised, and at every meeting the small yellow *PLEASE* leaflets were distributed to everyone present, and a *PLEASE* speech was an essential part of the proceedings. V.G. himself drew up the text of the *PLEASE* leaflet, and also of the four-page Prospectus, working over his drafts with the greatest care in order to secure the right response. He took immense pains with the Club speech, which could easily run to forty-five minutes, and which he delivered whenever he spoke at a Rally. He would work over it for hours, revising it and extending it as the occasion required, to put over the whole purpose of the Club. V.G. was a forceful and eloquent speaker, and he delivered his Club speech with tremendous conviction.

The *PLEASE* leaflets did not ask for enrolment, but only invited people to fill in their name and address so that they could receive by post particulars of the Club. In a meeting of 500 people, one could easily get two or three hundred *PLEASE* applications signed, and these would go immediately to Henrietta Street. The particulars of the Club would be sent, and the leaflet eventually passed on to the local group, which could then inform the sender of their next meeting for study, or of the next public meeting. So the Club grew. By April 1939 it had reached 57,000, and this remained the Club's highest membership figure.

An indispensable adjunct of the books was the *Left Book News* which soon became the *Left News*.[1] This had a variety of purposes : first, it gave all the necessary information about the Choices, and also about the Additional Books, the Supplementaries, the Educational Series (which in due course will be described) and whatever further projects stemmed from the enterprising brain and inexhaustible energy of V.G. Secondly, it contained the Editorial. V.G. asserted in the first issue that this would not appear again; that it had only been necessary to give the initial information! In fact it appeared in every issue and became an eloquent instrument of the Club's policy and aims, of its faith and its challenge. It was intensely personal. It was clear and fully informative (and it needed to be). It exhorted and it praised. It warned and it pleaded. It spurred to action. It unfolded new projects. The personality of V.G. could be

[1] In December, 1936.

felt on every page. It gave the Club its feeling of responsibility, of involving everyone in the movement. Thirdly, came the long review of the Book of the Month (and, later, of the Additional books). This made clear why the book had been chosen and what it was all about. Fourthly, it contained an article in a series designed to expand and explain the basic principles of the Club; the Popular Front, what was going on in Russia, the Fascist world offensive and so forth. Then came important documents: a speech on the Popular Front by Thorez; a speech by Maisky, the Russian Ambassador; a lengthy summary of the new Russian Constitution.

The number of groups grew rapidly, and the *Left Book News* began to play its part in guiding and developing them. In the autumn of 1936 I was asked to become the organiser of the groups and took over responsibility for this side of the Club. Succeeding issues of the *Left News* found a considerable number of pages dealing with the immense variety of group activities which rapidly developed. It soon became apparent that the groups had a function of their own: they discussed the books, they organised lectures and meetings. Soon we were sending the authors of the chosen books on nation-wide tours to lecture on their works—one of the first of these was given by Arthur Koestler on his *Spanish Testament,* one of the last by J. B. S. Haldane on *Air Raid Precautions.*

We now see the Club fairly launched: the first six books distributed and being read and discussed; a feeling, on the part of the members, of belonging to a movement; interest in the informative articles in the *Left News* by Laski, Strachey and other writers; and a growing response to the sense of urgency and excitement which characterised V.G.'s editorials.

The first major theme as it developed in these months was necessarily that of the menace of fascism and the urgent necessity for uniting and consolidating the progressive forces of democratic Europe to prevent the total disappearance of political freedom and the arrest of all social progress.

The menace was indeed terrifying. Hitler had finally disposed of all the political parties opposed to him in Germany. He was rapidly rearming. The Ruhr had been occupied, Austria engulfed. A stream of threats were directed against Russia— here was the "room for expansion" which would set German industry on its feet, he declared again and again. One by one the Eastern European powers succumbed to German penetration and domination. The Baltic republics were now dictatorships. Hungary, Rumania, Yugoslavia, Poland and Czechoslovakia were all threatened.

The League of Nations appeared powerless. Mussolini had invaded Abyssinia with no more than token protests to stop him. Spain was on the point of fascist revolt. Then came Franco's insurrection and the massive intervention on his behalf by Hitler and Mussolini. Crisis succeeded crisis. Each might have produced a war, but each in turn subsided as the democratic powers conceded demand after demand. In November, 1936, the threat of war grew darker with the signing of an Anti-Comintern pact between Germany and Japan. Meanwhile the two Axis Powers tightened their totalitarian system, and pushed on with the work of weakening the free nations by corrupting venal politicians—forming what the Spanish general marching on Madrid called a "fifth column" to disrupt the democratic government from within.

Tragically enough they profited at every turn of events from the powerful and growing pacifist movement in Britain. This had the influential support of Bertrand Russell, Aldous Huxley and C. E. M. Joad, whose books had a large circulation. The Peace Pledge Union, with its ideas of religious pacifism, in combination with the widespread Labour and progressive antagonism to conscription and rearmament, and the conviction of many socialists that (as an imperialist power) Britain was in no position to interfere with Mussolini or Hitler, all contributed to the reluctance to take any step which might provoke Hitler to war.

The Club devoted all its efforts to the explanation and advocacy of a People's Front, which was the real policy of the Club throughout its history. It was one of the main topics of the Club's public meetings, and of an important article by Strachey in the *Left Book News* for August 1936. A galaxy of speakers on this subject appeared at the Club meetings, their viewpoints extending across the whole political spectrum. There were Wilfrid Roberts, M.P., and Richard Acland, M.P., who spoke as Liberals; Robert Boothby was a Conservative; Harry Pollitt and Palme Dutt were Communists; Stafford Cripps, Aneurin Bevan, Russell Strauss and Ellen Wilkinson spoke for Labour; Eleanor

Rathbone was an Independent; Harold Laski was a Labour man and John Strachey belonged to no party but was closely associated with the Communists. And then there was the Dean of Canterbury and with him quite an influential and numerous body of progressive clergy of all denominations.

But Gollancz insisted that the Club was not, and would never become, a political party. It was rather a body of men and women of all parties, hammering out their difficulties and coming to agreement on certain immediate issues, and then acting in their various organisations to take effective action.

Nor was the Club the Popular Front in being. It was creating the kind of understanding and conviction out of which a coalition or Front of political entities and leaders could emerge. This possibility arose *out of the ideas* being discussed, but there was no obligation on any member to accept such a policy or any other policy as a condition of joining the club or participating in its activities.

What was continually stressed in those early days was the appeal to the members to accept political responsibility, to become active citizens playing their part in the affairs of the country and of the world, and therefore seeking the knowledge without which there can be no such responsible action.

But the Club was by no means concerned only with questions of war and peace. There was another war to fight and not to avoid—the war against poverty; and all those who stood for the People's Front, for Collective Security, stood also for the broad policies of socialist reform and reconstruction which formed the second plank in the Club's platform.

Our members were not even, as might be supposed, a number of thoughtful people of socialist and pacifist views, rather at odds with the Labour Party and partial to Communism. There were many such people and they played an active part in the groups, but the overwhelming majority were newcomers, non-politicals, worried and disturbed at the trend of events, dismayed and shocked at the overthrow of constitutional government in Spain, deeply concerned at the persisting poverty in the distressed areas of Britain. They ranged across the entire social scale. Groups were started among taxi drivers, railway workers at the London termini, in factories and trade unions, among medical students, and in Evening Institutes. Take any bus or tube on its way to town and in that cross-section of citizens you would see the Left Book Club. The majority were new to politics, or were only on the fringe. Coming in to seek information they found themselves shouldering new responsibilities, jerked out of the trivial round and general indifference to affairs. Life became significant for them and the books exciting reading.

We learnt a lot about this not only from the groups but from the enormous correspondence triggered by the Club. This delighted V.G. and he wrote hundreds of personal letters in reply. He begged all of us working with him never to send a brief and formal answer to a question or letter, but to respond warmly with offers of any further help we could give. Many letters were critical or asked for more light on the Club's aim, on the pacifist issue, on our relation to religion—were we atheists? Complaints came in that we were ignoring the Labour Party or not giving them a fair crack of the whip. Most letters were grateful, enthusiastic, deeply moving, as they told how inspiring and helpful the books had proved, and especially the new fellowship they had found in the groups.

What was a complete surprise was the awakening of interest among professional people, men of letters, poets, artists, actors and musicians. Actors for instance are not highly political as a rule, but very quickly a surprisingly large number of them gathered a group together which met in Great Newport Street at the Group Theatre.

Of course the meetings organised by these groups were not limited to Club members—non-members were welcomed; and the influence of the Club was greatly extended in this way.

In addition to the groups organised by actors, poets, writers, artists, and musicians, there were organised groups of journalists, lawyers, architectural students and commercial travellers.

In November, 1937, we received a letter from Essex which gives some idea of the kind of people who were involved in the groups :

> Our Group consists of a draughtsman, a doctor of physics, a printer, a bank clerk, a dental mechanic, a road mender, a school teacher, a painter, several clerks and sundry others. We have already contributed quite a lot to the building up of the local Labour Party. We have been able to get a scheme started for supporting a Basque child [a refugee from Spain] and have persuaded the Labour Party to run a film show in aid of Spain.

It should be realised that the Groups' Department at 14 Henrietta Street did not merely register these activities, but was extremely active in encouraging them, and visiting them.

Our aim was to have a group in every sizable town in England. In 1937 we published a list of the hundred towns in which there was still no group—appealed for members to get them going, and saw the list diminishing every week. Then we made a list of all the postal districts in London in which there was still no group, and one by one these gaps were filled too.

Some of the reports and letters which came pouring in gave us some idea of the composition of the groups. The Hackney Group consisted of

> 6 factory workers
> 1 railway guard
> 2 office workers
> 1 manager
> 2 bank clerks
> 1 analytical chemist
> 5 housewives.

In other districts the composition of the Groups might be more middle class, but Hackney was representative of the industrial areas and many parts of London. Groups now began to appear in hospitals (among the staff), in the Post Office, and in factories. A workshop group of twenty-four wrote in for advice. Someone wrote from Furness Vale, "We have a membership of thirty-two, which I suppose isn't bad for a village."

As time went on a feature of the group was the increasing use of 16 mm film : an organisation called Kino, which was ready to help us, took films round the country to be shown at group meetings. Eisenstein's *The Battleship Potemkin* was popular, and so was a moving film on *The Defence of Madrid,* as well as other films of the Spanish Civil War, which was now raging. But the first purpose of the groups was the systematic study of the book of the month.

It might be asked, how far were the books actually read? We have some interesting letters which throw light on this question. A young woman who worked at the L.M.S. Railway office in Somerstown told us how the office workers formed a group which purchased a copy each month and passed it round. She confessed that she didn't read much herself, but her boy friend, who was a socialist, certainly did. Interest livened up when the book that arrived one month was Dr E. F. Griffith's *Modern Marriage and Birth Control*! Another letter came from Hyde in Cheshire enclosing a stout exercise book containing a record of the weekly meetings of the Group and careful summaries of the contents of the monthly choices, with notes for lectures or discussion openings. This small group consisted of about a dozen members meeting in private houses weekly.

That the books were read pretty thoroughly by a fair number, and more cursorily by others, was shown by the attendance at the monthly discussions, by the correspondence, and by the marked development of interest and commitment in topics hitherto only the concern of political enthusiasts. There were vigorous debates, lively gatherings and large attendances at lectures, school and public meetings. The days when apathy prevailed, when no-one could be induced to come to meetings, were over. Such an awakening of interest and feeling of urgency and responsibility, however far it fell short of thorough knowledge of the facts and genuine understanding of the issues, was at any rate evidence of something essential to the meaning of democracy: an alive, alert, and interesting minority of people taking their citizenship seriously.

The existence of a large, ever-growing and lively membership already, during the first year of the Club's existence, organised into several hundred groups, opened up many possibilities of providing books over and above the monthly choices. Clearly there was a potential demand here from this intelligent and eager body of readers. As a consequence the Club began to produce various types of optional books which members taking the monthly choice could order if they wished. Before long they had the possibility of adding from two to six optional books each month as well as the regular choice.

The first of these were the Additional books. They were new, like the choice, but were generally selected from books already in the course of production for Gollancz's list. The additional book was announced in the *Left News* the month before publication, and had to be specially ordered by writing to Henrietta Street. Soon this method was abandoned, and the member had to order the book by filling in a card, and it was included with the choice when that was sent to the local bookseller who supplied the member. The first Additional book was G. C. M. M'Gonigle's *Poverty and Public Health,* about which we shall have a good deal to say when we discuss the Club's contribution to the question of poverty and unemployment. This was issued in August 1936.

Then came the Topical books which dealt with questions of special urgency. The idea was to produce very quickly a book either demanded by some critical situation or because some valuable material came unexpectedly to hand. This would be rushed out, and despatched by post to the subscriber instead of reaching him in the usual manner through his bookseller. The first of these was *The Nazi Conspiracy in Spain* by Otto Katz and it was published in January 1937. Seven books in this series were issued, the last being Eleanor Rathbone's *War Can Be Averted* (January 1938).

In the spring of 1937 came the first of the Supplementary books. They were books of real importance but of limited interest and not likely to be wanted by the whole membership. They too had to be ordered in advance on a card enclosed in the *Left News*. The Supplementaries began in May 1937 with two books : one on the pacifist question, *The Citizen Faces War* by Robert and Barbara Donington, and the second a symposium on *Christianity and the Social Revolution.*

Four reprints of books which had already made a name for themselves were issued as Reprints of the Classics. They were *The Town Labourer* by J. L. and B. Hammond, R. H. Tawney's *The Acquisitive Society,* Emile Burns' selections from Marx, Engels, Lenin and Stalin entitled *A Handbook of Marxism,* and John Strachey's *The Coming Struggle for Power.* Finally came the Educational series, but as this became associated with a new form of membership, we shall deal with it later. The first Educational was Emile Burns' *Money,* issued in July 1937. These were short popular books which assumed "no previous knowledge whatever on the part of the reader." They dealt with a great variety of topics and cost only sixpence to members of the Club.

There were now several cards of various colours which were included in the *Left News* and this complexity and abundant flood of published material became something of a joke.

Something must be said about the machinery of distribution, which was in itself an organisational matter of some initial difficulty which demanded very careful handling. The primary aim was to get the books distributed by the booksellers and to avoid by-passing them by direct despatch through the mail. There was a good deal of suspicion and downright opposition to overcome on the part of some booksellers, but in the long run they found that they were able to carry out the distribution at a reasonable profit.[2] Under this scheme all bills were payable to the bookseller, not to Victor Gollancz Limited. Members picked up the books when notified by postcard that the choice had arrived, or could arrange with the bookseller to have their copies posted to them.

Members who had no convenient bookseller available were supplied by two London bookshops, the Phoenix Book Company, the first bookshop to publicise the Club, and the Workers' Bookshop. At this time Left-wing bookshops were springing up all over Britain and they naturally played an important part in distributing the books. Many of them were able to establish themselves financially largely on account of distributing the books; and then they provided a centre for the sale of other progressive literature to the new readership created by the Club.

Every book issued by the Club had printed on the cover

LEFT BOOK CLUB EDITION
NOT FOR SALE TO THE PUBLIC

This was, of course, necessary from the standpoint of the trade, but it sometimes aroused the darkest suspicions of subversive intentions behind the Club's activities. Under-the-counter schemes to circulate forbidden literature were detected in this mysterious notice. In fact of course every such book was also issued by Victor Gollancz Ltd, in full cloth binding—at two or three times the Club price of half a crown. And the editions for the general public sold very well indeed at this price. But for the Club members it meant that for the first time the books they needed and wanted were available at a price within the reach of most people's pockets.

V.G. was always on the alert to recognise weak places in the methods of the Club. One of the first of these he found to be the sheer burden of reading a book a month, some of them long, some of them difficult. The books tended to accumulate

[2] The bookseller received the usual discount of one-third off the retail price of half a crown.

in a reproachful row on the bookshelf, too many of them only glanced through, not read. Members, only a few, but still potential and willing readers, gave up and resigned.

V.G. at once took measures to save this lapse and recover the lost members. In the Autumn of 1937 he created a new category of membership—the "B" members. They received their choice only every other month; and the planning of the successive choices saw to it that it was the shortest, easiest and most popular book that appeared in the B members' month. Once again, as for the regular membership, the minimum obligation of membership was for six months. Although the B members received the *Left News* each month, they had to pay more for the books they received—this was at first three shillings and sixpence, but in January 1938 it was reduced to three shillings.

V.G. then came to the conclusion that there were still many people who could be induced to buy and read the Club books regularly, even though not six in the year. Why not offer only *four* books a year at half a crown, but *not* the *Left News*? These were the "C" members. In the event B and C members accounted for ten per cent of the whole;[3] meanwhile the regular membership continued steadily and rapidly to increase.

[3] *Left News* (September 1938).

CHAPTER III

THE FIRST YEAR

1936–1937

At the end of May 1937, after one year of its existence, the Club membership reached 44,800. It was a year of experiment as well as growth. Neither V.G. nor the other selectors, Strachey and Laski, had anticipated the developments which actually occurred. Some of the books were to become classics in their own right.

"When we started the Club we had no idea of its potentialities," wrote Gollancz in the May 1937 issue of the *Left News*. He proposed resolutely to seize the opportunity offered by this rapid growth and the widespread enthusiasm it had aroused.

> We must take full advantage of it, we must follow up and consolidate every development. It is a matter partly of organisation, partly of constantly adding to our staff people particularly suited for particular jobs. I only want to say here that we are alive to the necessity of spending most of our waking hours in devising new methods of dealing with our problems.

This pointed to the main activities of the coming years: recruiting new members, organising public lectures and meetings, awakening the interest of wider circles, largely professional, and broad sections of the general public up to now largely indifferent to political questions.

In the first issue of the *Left Book News* (May 1936), Gollancz had first expressed the hope that the Club would attract "the very many who, being fundamentally well disposed, hold aloof from the fight by reason of ignorance or apathy". Before there was any kind of propaganda organisation, beyond the leaflets, any group activity, or any lectures and public meetings, it was only the books themselves that reached those who we hoped and expected would respond—and they did.

It was the books selected and published during the first year that set the Club on its feet. The first month's choice as we have mentioned was *France Today and the People's Front* by Maurice Thorez, General Secretary of the French Communist Party, and as a companion volume a book on the genetic future of man, *Out of the Night* by Professor H. J. Muller. Thorez set out to show how the very real threat of a Fascist coup in France was met and defeated because of the instant reaction of the French working-class movement, and above all its unity; whereas in Germany a divided working-class movement had been able to offer no effective resistance to Hitler.

This was immediately followed by *Hitler the Pawn* by Rudolf Olden, formerly Political Editor of the *Berliner Tageblatt*. He did not offer a Marxist interpretation of Hitler's rise to power, but simply gave the record of his life. "The truth is,' wrote Strachey in his review, "that Olden writes from a purely, and indeed narrowly, liberal point of view." Then came R. Palme Dutt's *World Politics, 1918–1936*. This book, written from a communist standpoint, tried to make sense of the whole complex development between the wars of capitalism in crisis, fascist reaction, and the trend towards a world war. The book suggested that the fascist powers could only be resisted and defeated by an alliance between the capitalist democracies and the Soviet Union. The choice for October was *Under the Axe of Fascism,* by the Italian Liberal, Gaetano Salvemini, who had been a Professor of History in Florence. This was a careful and thoroughly documented study of Mussolini's claims tested against performance. It was by no means a piece of fiery denunciation, nor was it popular in style. It raised protests from some members as "too difficult". V.G. published these letters, and immediately other readers wrote in to urge V.G. not to let down the high standard of the choices. They liked some tough material. It reflected the serious educational character of the Club, which was not brought into existence, they declared, to promote light reading.

Continuing for the moment to note the sequence of books concerned with the struggle against Fascism, we come to the choice for December 1936, *Spain in Revolt* by two American journalists, Gannes and Repard. The Spanish Civil War was to become the first issue which really stirred the conscience and quickened the political understanding of those hitherto not particularly interested in politics. Here was a workmanlike and sound piece of reporting, but by no means a full and authoritative account of the complex Spanish situation. It was important because it brought home to the Club the significance of reaction against democracy that was being supported by the intervention of Fascist Italy and Nazi Germany. The little Topical book, *The Nazi Conspiracy in Spain,* published in January 1937, revealed the deliberate steps taken by Hitler to secure the victory for Franco, by sending the Condor Legion to Spain. Another (Topical) book, which anticipated, some years before it happened, the bombing of Britain, was *The Protection of the Public from Aerial Attack* by a group of Cambridge scientists.

In December 1937 came another important book on Spain by Arthur Koestler, *Spanish Testament,* with which the author made his name. This gave a first hand picture of the early days of the Civil War as it appeared to him and a moving account of his imprisonment with many others who subsequently went to their execution, while he narrowly escaped.

It was not until June 1938 that Frank Jellinek's scholarly, balanced book, *The Civil War in Spain,* appeared as an Additional book. It is very rare indeed to secure a book written in the heat and turmoil of such events that can be expected to reveal the reality behind them. As Hegel said, we understand only *after* the event when it is often too late to do much about it.

The influence of the Spanish Civil War was undoubtedly very great. Volunteers from many countries joined the International Brigades. Many brilliant writers, poets and university students lost their lives in Spain—one recalls John Cornford, Ralph Fox, Christopher Caudwell. At home there was a massive campaign on behalf of Franco. Without the aid of the Club, it is doubtful if the other side would have been heard to much effect. As V.G. wrote later, "while there was no official censorship in this country, in fact there was an invisible barrier across which it was almost impossible to get progressive literature into the hands of the general public."[1]

The Club made its first public impact on Spain. It organised rallies and raised money for medical aid. It stocked

[1] *Left News* (August 1945).

and launched a food ship. The groups studied the books, and invited speakers on Spain to address public meetings.

But the Club books did not deal exclusively with the menace of Fascism and the danger of war. One of the most successful and popular of the books published in the first year was Wilfrid Macartney's *Walls have Mouths*. Written from his own experience in prison it is said to have been instrumental in reforming the prison system in certain directions. We thus come to the books which were concerned with "a better social and economic order", which in the *Left News* editorials and other Club pronouncements became more and more explicitly the presentation of socialism as the most effective path to social reform for most of the Club members. This was the theme of Stephen Spender's *Forward from Liberalism,* the choice for January 1937.

The choice for April 1937 was Leo Huberman's *Man's Worldly Goods*. This was a remarkably effective piece of popularisation which attempted to give a rapid survey of the last six hundred years of social and economic history. It added to the factual picture something of a philosophy of history from the Marxist point of view. Laski wrote in his review in the *Left News,* "No effective programme of the Left is possible without a philosophy of history. Upon its basis there can be built an insight into our present discontents of immense value to the movement we represent."

One of the most popular of the books on social problems was George Orwell's *The Road to Wigan Pier* (March, 1937), the sales of which reached over 40,000. Orwell, with great expertise, did for our time what Dickens and Zola had done for theirs : he brought home to the sleeping imagination the real lives of suffering men and women.

John Strachey had always been one of the most influential speakers and writers for the Club, as well as a selector. Profoundly interested in political theory, he had also a strong desire to take part in practical activities. Moreover, he was a Marxist who could expound his theories without a trace of dogmatism.

Before the Club had been formed he had written *The Coming Struggle for Power,* followed by an important book *The Nature of Capitalist Crisis*. Then came *The Meaning of Fascism* which, more than any other book devoted to the perils and complexities of a confused world, not only described but explained the significance of fascism. Now he produced, as the choice for November 1936, *The Theory and Practice of Socialism*. Before the publication of this book there had hardly been a single comprehensive popular exposition of socialism since Blatchford's *Britain for the British* (1900). It at once became immensely popular. It may be as well to note at this point that the books issued by the Club were never regarded by the selectors, the readers, or the speakers of consequence who supported the Club, as some kind of orthodox pronouncement or formulation which carried unanimous approval. Laski criticised Strachey's book for its inadequate treatment of the State, and for sliding over certain difficulties in the theory of dialectical materialism, nor was he entirely convinced by the economic arguments. But he concluded his review by declaring that Strachey

has given us a superb introduction to the understanding of Marxism, a restatement of its essence that is clear, incisive and challenging. He has done his part admirably. It now remains for us to see that its lesson penetrates into every nook and cranny of the movement.[2]

Strachey's *Theory and Practice of Socialism* was well written and closely argued. The Club proceeded to set up a Training School for group leaders who would be prepared to go out to the groups and take study courses on the book over a period of four or five weeks. Lectures on it were given by all the Club topline speakers over the whole country. And there was also Strachey himself, who addressed a great many meetings on his own book.

I suppose no single book more completely fulfilled the basic aim of the Club: to provide that disciplined study, rooted in fact and illuminated by theory, which was what the Club wanted to give its members. It stiffened the fibres of a Club whose sympathetic feeling and genuine passion needed precisely this basic *understanding* of the forces at work in capitalist civilisation.

In the first year of the Club, while the Labour Party was less than enthusiastic, there was little opposition, and Clement Attlee was sympathetic enough to send a message to the first

[2] *Left Book News* (November 1936).

Albert Hall Rally in February 1937 and to write the Club choice for August 1937, *The Labour Party in Perspective*. This book was important because of the position and influence of Attlee in the Labour party, but it proved to be an uninspiring and an unpopular choice. In fact the Labour Party leadership became increasingly hostile to the Club and furious that Labour men like Stafford Cripps, Aneurin Bevan and Harold Laski should appear on the same platform at Club meetings with Harry Pollitt. But its members joined the Club in large numbers, and even the local Party organisations frequently co-operated warmly with the groups. Eventually, worried at the influence of the Club books, the Labour Party started its own Labour Book Service.

To conclude this review of the books published by the Club in its first year, it is interesting to note the books which ranged beyond the immediate political and social issues. For instance the second month of the Club's existence saw two novels as the choice : *Days of Contempt* by André Malraux, and *Choose a Bright Morning* by Hillel Bernstein. They were not very popular. In March 1937 the choice was *Freud and Marx* by Reuben Osborn, a not altogether successful attempt to relate the theories of Freud to those of Marx. Then there were two political atlases by J. F. Horrabin, the brilliant cartographer and the illustrator of Wells' *Outline of History*. They were *An Atlas of Current Affairs,* and *An Atlas of Empire*. Both were Additional books.

In February 1937, the Choice was Frank Jellinek's *The Paris Commune of 1871*,[3] an excellent example of the more scholarly type of book issued from time to time, but it was also one that had some contemporary relevance. The events of 1871 were by no means treated in a spirit of revolutionary romanticism. On the contrary it was a sober historical study which really assumed that the reader knew something about the brief story of the uprising. It was strictly academic, factually accurate and, for the ordinary reader at that time, a rather difficult book. For the purposes of Club members, it needed a synopsis and some explanatory commentary. This was supplied by a brilliant woman historian Dona Torr.

However it so happened that someone managed to get hold

[3] To be reissued by Victor Gollancz Ltd. in 1971 with a new Foreword.

of a set of slides made from actual photographs of the uprising; and we also found a very curious, exciting and highly obscure film about the Commune called *The New Babylon*. The groups who were fortunate enough to use these, worked up some excellent meetings round them, and some even found a competent historian to lecture on the Commune at the same time; thus a difficult book would be presented in an attractive way.

The difficulties of some books, and the complexity and richness of the material in others, such as *The Theory and Practice of Socialism,* made the provision of study outlines by the Groups Department a necessity; and these were produced each month and reached all conveners and those prepared to lecture on the books or open discussions.

After the first Albert Hall Rally we held a conference of conveners attended by 190 delegates (120 conveners and 70 group representatives). The result was a wealth of suggestion as to ways of working, and much valuable insight into how the books were being received, read and discussed. When conveners realised that all over the country groups like their own were to be found and were flourishing they were greatly encouraged. The conference was a landmark in the development of the groups.

The *Left News* came to play an increasing part in the life of the Club. Starting with fifteen pages, by the end of the year it had grown to thirty. On the first few pages came all the announcements : first of the choice for the next month, then of the Additional and Supplementary books. April, 1937, had a whole page explaining the Topical books. Later the procedure for obtaining the Educational books appeared.

All the books, issued or to be issued, were fully reviewed—the choice in the same month as its publication, the Additional books the month before. Many of these reviews were by Professor Laski. Strachey wrote the "Topic of the Month", on such questions as "Collective Security", "A People's Front for Britain", or "The Civil War in Spain". In September 1937, he wrote a strong appeal to the Labour Party in connection with the Autumn Conference at Bournemouth. Rejoicing at the new spirit of militancy that was beginning to emerge among the rank and file, Strachey urged Labour to realise that the road to success in its domestic policy lay in grappling firmly with the problem of poverty caused by wages lagging behind the rise in prices. But he pointed out that such home problems were bound up with Labour's foreign policy, and that "the Labour Movement cannot advance unless it now exerts its whole power to prevent the British Government from betraying world peace and world democracy to fascism."

The *Left News* not only printed the names and addresses of the group conveners, but published notices of group meetings, lectures and week-end schools. By April, 1937, there were five pages of such material, and there were now between 400 and 500 groups.

The Editorials by Victor Gollancz were always the first thing one turned to after the Announcements. They were valuable for the political lead they gave the Club and for their sense of urgency and commitment. They recorded and inspired every new development of the Club; quoted and replied to letters from members; exhorted and sometimes rebuked. They gave to the Club that immediate feeling of personal direction, of burning enthusiasm, of deep interest and involvement in every aspect of Club work and of the activities of the groups, which gave the Club its unity and sense of mission.

The event of the year was the Albert Hall Rally on February 7th, 1937. The hall was completely sold out. The speakers were John Strachey, Richard Acland, M.P., Professor Laski, D. N. Pritt, K.C., M.P., Harry Pollitt, and, of course, Victor Gollancz, who was in the Chair.

V.G. opened the proceedings by reading greetings from members and friends of the Club all over the world—from Johannesburg and Colombo, from Zurich and Mauritius, from Western Australia and Auckland. Then came a message from Attlee, the Leader of the Labour Party (which was not long to continue its support), and an unexpected telegram from Jawaharlal Nehru of India.

The speakers, from political positions as wide apart as Acland's Liberalism and Pollitt's Communism, were cheerfully frank about their differences, but unanimous as to their agreement on the basic issues of the Popular Front. One could best capture the spirit of the Rally by key quotations from the speeches rather than from an attempt to summarise them.

Victor Gollancz said that the Club was neither a political party, nor was it the Popular Front, but "we are creating the

mass basis without which no true Popular Front is possible."
Speaking of the groups he said that one of the remarkable things
which had emerged from them was the discovery "of completely
new political talent which, I think, but for the Left Book Club,
might have remained completely undiscovered."

John Strachey said :

"There are millions of people in this country still who do not
realise that what is happening in Spain today is of deadly
concern to them . . .

"I believe that the Fascist world-offensive is an inevitable,
determinate consequence, in the last analysis, of the particular
way in which the economic life of five-sixths of the world is
arranged today.

"If you organise your economic life so that certain countries
that have come too late in the competitive struggle, are forced
by their ruling classes to attempt to re-divide the world, in doing
so they will plunge the world into another blood bath."

Professor Laski saw the Club as not so much a mass movement as an educational body and a minority movement :

"Since I spend the major part of my life in that state of
resentful coma, that in the Universities we call research . . . I
will plead with the members of the Left Book Club always to
insist that the standards we have set in this Club are invariably
and continuously right . . . I want from our movement to come
the inspiration that makes for knowledge."

D. N. Pritt, K.C., M.P., spoke of the hunger of the workers
for good political literature, and the urgent necessity for the
Labour Party to find "a real foundation of doctrine, of understanding, of philosophy, of history and experience to our socialist
thoughts . . . Therefore let us encourage ourselves to get over
the natural formlessness of the English mind and build up a real
Socialist education."

Harry Pollitt saw the inevitability of disagreement in the Club
on many questions as well as unity on the basic principles of
struggle against Fascism. That would be a good thing. "There is
not sufficient discussion on the British movement, there is not
sufficient hammering out of differences, there is not sufficient

explaining of various points of view, and the function of this Club is that it clarifies and clears the air."

Pollitt concluded by quoting something that Lenin said in the early days of the Revolution : and it might well be the best expression of the hopes and fears of the Club at the end of the first year of its life.

"We have only just obtained the opportunity of learning. I do not know how long this opportunity will last. But every moment we have free from war we must devote to study."[4]

[4] Lenin, 1921.

CHAPTER IV

THE YEAR OF ACHIEVEMENT

1937–1938

IN THE *Left News* for September 1938, Victor Gollancz wrote :

> When the history of the Left Book Club comes to be written
> there will be found I think, to be five landmarks in its history.
> 1 The foundation of the first group a month or so after the
>   foundation of the Club itself.
> 2 The Albert Hall Rally of February, 1937.
> 3 The formation of the Left Book Club Theatre Guild later
>   in the same year.
> 4 The rapid springing up of Club premises during the Spring of
>   1938.
> 5 The phenomenal distribution by the membership of the Club
>   itself of Strachey's pamphlet : *Why You Should be a Socialist.*
> These will stand out as the milestones on our road.

In his Editorial in the *Left News* for May 1937, Victor
Gollancz opened with his "Anniversary Self-Criticism". He
wanted a membership of not 50,000 but 100,000. With that,
he wrote, "we should be, I believe, the most powerful body of
educated public opinion that any country has ever had." It
would be possible, he continued, if every "ordinary" member
became an "extraordinary" member "taking an active part in
the affairs of the Club by recruiting, joining their local group,
fitting themselves to be leaders of discussions, and so on and
so forth." It was precisely the very great achievements of the
first year that opened up tremendous possibilities.

> The never ceasing development of the Club has, so to speak,
> taken our breath away . . . we live in a real fear that this mar-
> vellous opportunity having occurred, we are not taking advantage

of it. And we *must* take full advantage of it—we must follow up and consolidate every development and seize every opportunity.

On the Agenda for the coming year we gave priority to the new "Educational" series, the development of Club premises and the Left Book Club Theatre Guild. The first Conference of Religious Leaders was announced. The books, now the subject of "scientific planning", were to include the important series on the problems of British Labour, which we have already mentioned, Robert Brady's *The Spirit and Structure of German Fascism*, due in September, and Edgar Snow's *Red Star Over China,* for October. V.G. explained that books take a long time to write and a certain amount of time to publish. In the early days of the Club the programme could not be the result of long distance planning, but now books were being *commissioned* well in advance, by the best authors possible on the topics about which the Club members ought to have information.

The groups expanded rapidly during the first full year of the Club's existence : they increased their range of special membership, they acquired premises or Club rooms, the Theatre Guild, and a whole range of other new ventures were started, including the first Summer School.

There now began to appear more Specialist Groups, as we called them. London Art Students, Paddington Railway Workers, Librarians, a Dance & Drama Group. There was even a group in the offices of the *Manchester Guardian*. One member organised a Corresponding Group of people who wanted to get in touch with other readers by post, often because they were isolated, and 150 members were found correspondents in this year.

One of the first and most popular Socialist weeklies had been the *Clarion* under the editorship of Robert Blatchford, a brilliant propagandist for socialism and the author of *Britain for the British* and *Merry England*. Readers of his paper had formed the Clarion Cycling Club which continued to flourish long after Blatchford's death. The Club soon organised an active group of the Left Book Club.

There was a Musicians Group which included Warwick Braithwaite, Arnold Goldsbrough, Edward Clark, Sidney Harrison, Alan Bush and also members of the London Philharmonic Orchestra, the B.B.C. Orchestra, Dance Band Leaders, composers, arrangers, solo artists and students. The musicians frequently made their own special contribution to Club events by performing for us at meetings, organising choirs, and writing songs. They were largely responsible for the successful evening programmes of music, poetry and lectures on cultural matters at the Summer Schools.

In March, 1938, the Club issued *The Left Song Book* edited by Alan Bush and Randall Swingler. It contained a number of traditional songs of freedom and revolt both from Britain and other countries and "Five Famous Rounds" with new words. They were arranged so that they could be sung in unison with piano and as part songs for mixed voices.

The Writers and Readers Group was particularly lively and included Cecil Day Lewis, Stephen Spender, Sylvia Townsend Warner, Rex Warner, Montagu Slater, Arthur Calder Marshall, Randall Swingler and many others.

It would be fitting to conclude this account of the cultural work of the Club in this year with a note on the Nottingham Celebration of the Byron Centenary. At this event the literary critic, Alick West, was the Public Orator. The Club designed a special banner for the occasion, including a portrait of the poet and the famous lines from "Childe Harold" :

> Yet, Freedom ! yet thy banner,
>   torn, but flying,
> Streams like the thunder-storm
>   *against* the wind.

The second Albert Hall Rally took place on January 16th 1938, at the Albert Hall, with the overflow at the Queen's Hall. Paul Robeson sang and newcomers to the platform were Sir Charles Trevelyan and Dr Christopher Addison (later Lord Addison) who was responsible for the agricultural policy of the Labour Party. This was followed by a series of rallies covering the whole country, taking the largest halls available in Manchester, Birmingham, Hull, Sheffield, Glasgow, Edinburgh, Newcastle, Stoke-on-Trent and Leeds.

Seven big meetings were also organised for London in Battersea Town Hall, the People's Palace, Hornsey Town Hall and so forth.

It was clear that the Club was now by far the largest and most enthusiastic political movement in the country. It was recruiting all the time; and its members found that here was an organisation actively inviting their co-operation, engaged in weekly lectures and discussions and a great variety of cultural activities, film shows, concerts and plays. And playing an important part in these regular activities were the increasing number of permanent Left Book Club premises or centres.

These Club rooms and small halls, which became a feature of the Club in its first year, had, by the end of the second, been established in some twenty-two towns. Wherever this happened the groups developed rapidly. Social gatherings, concerts and plays took place—refreshment could be made available. The group could now become an organisation with a considerable range of cultural activities. One of the best equipped was the Leeds Centre, with its library, small stage, kitchen and committee rooms. Its Forum had a subscribing membership of 200, and the premises were open every night of the week. It was a popular place for debates and political training classes.

The Paddington premises consisted of the upper rooms of a large house in Sutherland Avenue. There was an admirably furnished club room with easy chairs and bookshelves, a room for meetings holding 40 or 50 people, two large committee rooms, and a buffet.

Cambridge and Camden Town, Chichester and Gloucester were among other groups with well-equipped Centres. It was a delightful experience when visiting one of these groups to drop in at a pleasantly furnished club room with a library, its evidence of constant use for gatherings of members, its atmosphere of people belonging, of fellowship.

Wolverhampton group owned a "Barn" formerly approached by a ladder—a cobwebby and gloomy place; but with a staircase, warmed and lighted, black beams and cheerful curtains and floor covering, this became a much frequented club room, used for socials as well as discussion and lectures, for play rehearsals, and for table tennis.

The Left Book Club Theatre Guild was a movement, energetically and successfully run by John Allen, which set up some 250 amateur companies in connection with the groups, putting on plays by such dramatists as Elmer Rice and Clifford Odets. They organised a Theatre Festival (with twenty-two entries), and a Summer School at Leiston with a syllabus covering all aspects of practical work, and with André van Gyseghem as resident lecturer.

The *Left News* recorded the steady growth of this work; and one can see how successfully it developed the suggestion made by C. Day Lewis, that we should supplement the educational work of the Club through drama. Where a group possessed premises, especially a small hall, the Guild was greatly helped and could link its creative work with the discussion groups and lectures based on the books. A great many short plays concerning Spain naturally appeared in these years.

One should not forget the part played by the little Unity Theatre in Goldington Street, St. Pancras, which was eager to offer us all possible help in everything concerning the Left Theatre and the Theatre Guild in those days. Here Paul Robeson himself acted without fee; here the clever satirical "Musical" on Chamberlain—*The Babes in the Wood,* drew crowded and hilarious audiences, and here young working-class actors like Bill Rowbotham and Alfie Bass began a semi-professional career that ended on the professional stage.

The Theatre Guild was in fact organised from Unity Theatre. Groups could affiliate for half a crown a year and the Guild did everything possible to guide the formation and development of amateur companies and to provide suitable plays for performance in small halls, using little in the way of scenery and costumes. Commencing in May 1937, by August 150 groups were in touch with the Guild. By the end of the year branches at Manchester, Liverpool, Glasgow, Cambridge and several other towns had performed one-act plays and sketches.

One of the most popular was Clifford Odets' *Waiting for Lefty.* Of the many other Left-wing plays, most of them forgotten, Herbert Hodge's *Where's that Bomb?* was a delightfully funny political skit; Jack Lindsay wrote frequently for the Guild, including *On Guard for Spain,* for mass recitation. George Fullard, an unemployed Sheffield miner, wrote *Clogs.*

A particularly interesting kind of performance was "The Living Newspaper" which vividly depicted the events of the day. Simon Blumenfeld's play *Enough of all This,* the story of a rent strike, was performed in the open air at Sunderland, where such a strike was in progress, to audiences hundreds strong.

In 1938 the Guild moved to the new office of the groups in Henrietta Street, where Paul Eisler and Meg Wintringham ran it until War came. Here they started the journal *Theatre for the People*. Paul Eisler was a young Czech refugee who became closely associated with the Club and often addressed group meetings. He worked as Organising Secretary of the Guild until War broke out. Although then only in his very early twenties, Paul's brilliant intellect and warm human personality enabled him to make a great contribution to the work of the Club. Shortly afterwards he was interned. On his release he served in the Czech Army until the end of the War. He married Jean Layton, the daughter of Sir Walter Layton of the *News Chronicle,* and after the War returned to Czechoslovakia. Here, after a period in limbo, working in a factory, he became a Professor of Economics and was actively concerned with the new economic policies advocated by Dubcek. To the profound grief of all who knew him, he died in a mountain accident in Switzerland in 1966.

By this time there were 250 branches of the Guild, associated with the groups, and they were playing a very useful role in their general activities, attracting people who might not in the first instance come to lectures but would enjoy a clever satire on contemporary events, or one of the topical plays, often of a high quality, which the Theatre Guild put on.

The story of the year's work must include the record of several new ventures. First of all there was a special meeting in the Queen's Hall[1] on April 19th, 1938, for non-members. Tickets were distributed by members to any non-members they could persuade to take them. Strachey spoke on Socialism, and Richard Acland, as a Liberal, spoke on Social Reform and the international situation. These were sober, informative lecture-discussions for the unconverted.

The hall was packed. Gollancz regarded this meeting as the greatest success yet registered by the Club. It began in a cool, if not rather hostile atmosphere. As the speakers began to deal with their themes it became clear that as well as the non-members a considerable body of fascists had invaded the meeting with the object of breaking it up. The result was not what they expected. As Richard Acland steadily, and without anger or confusion, continued in quietly reasonable tones, the sympathy of the entire

[1] The old Queen's Hall in Portland Place which was the main London concert hall before the War. It was destroyed by bombs and replaced by the Festival Hall.

audience with the exception of the fascists, came over to his side. The "climate" of the audience changed before our eyes. It quickly became apparent that the fascists had grotesquely miscalculated. Applause for Club speakers became more and more widespread and enthusiastic. As the meeting went on the disheartened fascists fell silent; several of them slunk out. Their attempt to wreck the meeting collapsed.

Finally, we had that year the first of our Summer Schools, at Digswell Park, Welwyn. This lovely park of 300 acres with a swimming pool, tennis courts and shady gardens, was ideal for the fortnight's school. We had lectures in the mornings—solid courses by, among others, G. D. H. Cole, Strachey, and by Horsfall Carter on Spain. Our early evening lectures on Russia were by Professor Bernal, A. S. Neill of Summerhill, Sir Walter Layton, D. N. Pritt, and by Professor Marrack on Soviet Medicine. The school was full to capacity.

A feature of the school was the after-supper programme of the Arts. Here poets read their work, novelists discussed the question of the relation of their work to society; Arthur Calder Marshall spoke on literature, and Sylvia Townsend Warner on the novel, the London Musicians played for us, and there was a film show by Kino, and a lecture on play production for amateurs by Monica Ewer.

The Club had published as a supplementary book a special edition of *Christianity & The Social Revolution,* which I edited for an editorial board consisting of Canon Charles Raven, Professor J. MacMurray and Dr Joseph Needham, and previously published in 1935. It was a precursor of the Christian Marxist Dialogue of our own time. Essays by W. H. Auden, Father Conrad Noel, John Cornford, Professor Pascal, a Russian contributor, John MacMurray and several others, stated the case as seen by one group from the Christian point of view, and by the other from the Marxist. V.G. was at pains when he issued it to declare that it was not intended to represent the unanimous views of the selectors. This warning was hardly necessary since the book by its very aim and professed intent represented sixteen different views.

Very many letters were received from people concerned about the religious problems raised in this book and by the deeper questions with which the Club was concerned. Many ministers of religion appeared on our platforms and attended our discussions. In June 1937 we decided to call a Conference of religious leaders on "Christianity & Socialism". Members came up from all over the country. I took the Chair and the opening speakers were Kenneth Ingram, a well-known Anglo-Catholic lawyer, Canon Narborough, and the Dean of Canterbury. It was more successful than we dared to hope, and we at once suggested to the groups that they should invite members of the Churches to work with them whenever suitable subjects arose.

Gollancz took this up in the *Left News* for August 1937.

There are many thousands of Christian people who are potential Allies of the Left rather than of the Right. Recent events in Germany have shown what an implacable foe fascism is to every form of Christianity. It is the aim of the Left Book Club to link up all the forces of progress and not to confine its unifying work to those who are already socialists. Just as we welcome non-socialists into the Club so we should extend our fellowship through religious conferences to the many thousands of Christian folk who are deeply concerned about the present crisis and as desirous as we are of averting war and fascism and building a new social order.

The response was warm enough to persuade us to launch a *Christian Book Club* under the editorship of the Dean of Canterbury. The plan was to issue four books during the year at prices ranging from 2/- to 3/6. It would be an integral part of the Left Book Club.

In July, 1937, immediately after the first Conference on Religion and Socialism, we issued as an Additional Book, a Canadian Symposium *Towards the Christian Revolution*, edited by Dr Gregory Vlastos, a well-known theologian. It was, however, not before July 1938 that the title of the first book for the Christian Book Club was announced. It was to be the Dean of Chichester's *Struggle for Religious Freedom in Germany*. This I reviewed in the *Left News* for that month.

Christian Groups were already coming into being, and by the Autumn of 1937 were established in London, Bath, Bolton, Birmingham, Greenock, Newcastle, Ramsgate, Torquay, Middlesbrough and Cambridge. Four groups were started in

London, under the influence of Kenneth Ingram and the well-known Quaker, Dorothy Buxton.

The last news from the Christian Groups was recorded in the January, 1938, issue of the *Left News*; after that we heard from time to time of their existence, but they did not grow in numbers and further books were not produced. It was a venture that never really got off the ground.

A number of the Club choices were philosophical books. First, Professor Levy's *A Philosophy for a Modern Man*. This was a daring *choice,* and not a Supplementary, as might be expected. Levy was sent on a lecture tour round the groups to explain his book. He was a brilliant speaker and a considerable wit. He aroused great interest everywhere and people turned to the book with high expectations—which were by no means always satisfied. The book was as tough and recondite as the lectures were racy and delightful.

A rather different book was *A Textbook of Marxist Philosophy*, edited and translated by myself and Arthur Moseley (Additional). It appeared in May 1937. This was a difficult but extremely interesting book and somewhat of a challenge to current over-simplifications of Dialectical Materialism. In November 1937, my little *Introduction to Philosophy* was published in the Educational Series.

Among the several hundred books published, and read by thousands, were not a few of more permanent value than the slighter but necessary tracts for the time like the books on the Spanish Civil War or the unemployed struggles in Britain. A great venture of genuine political education had been started which continued long after the last Left Book Club choice was issued, for its books were still read and their influence spread from mind to mind.

These activities, largely concerned with the home front, went on against a background of passionate involvement in international affairs. In June *Hitler's Conspiracy Against Peace*, by S. Erckner, appeared as an Additional book, and in September the long awaited *Spirit and Structure of German Fascism* by Robert A. Brady. The reprint of Strachey's *The Coming Struggle for Power*, first published in 1933, made available to a still larger readership his diagnosis of the sickness of capitalist society and the alternatives which the Marxist saw confronting Western man. The Independent Member of Parliament, Eleanor Rathbone, wrote the Topical book *War Can Be Averted,* another plan for effective collective security.

The situation in Europe, already critical, had worsened. Spain was in the throes of a revolt of the army against the constitutional government. This caused deep anxiety everywhere and especially among members of the Club. After the publication of *Spain in Revolt* by Gannes and Repard in December 1936, sympathy for the Republic grew among the club members, the Liberal and Labour parties, and among the more alert of the general public.

The Spanish question far transcended politics in the ordinary sense. For the generation of the thirties the controversy provided the emotional experience of a lifetime. No foreign question since the French Revolution had so profoundly appealed to the deepest human instincts and democratic feelings.

Nowhere was this intense feeling more passionate and urgent than in the Club. Every group now entered into the struggle, endeavouring to understand the whole situation, and then organising medical aid and bringing the maximum pressure on the Government to prevent military intervention by Germany and Italy, and to allow the legitimate government of Spain to purchase arms.

Our first task was to enable members to grasp the full meaning of what was going on. The Club provided the facts, the comments, the explanatory articles in the *Left News* and the organisation to develop and seek appropriate action for this awakening of mind and conscience. The *Left News* issued two special numbers on Spain containing articles by Alvarez del Vayo, Laski, Stafford Cripps and John Strachey.

From January 5th to January 17th, 1938, Arthur Koestler toured the country speaking on his book *Spanish Testament.* Koestler had been present at some of the desperate encounters of the war, including the fall of Malaga, and was imprisoned by the fascists and for months was in danger of his life. He visited Portsmouth, Taunton, Plymouth, Gloucester, Cheltenham, Birmingham, Stoke-on-Trent, Leicester, Lincoln, Bradford, Blyth, Accrington, Southport, Liverpool and Manchester.

In the January, 1938, *Left News*—the second special Spain number—Gollancz rallied the Club membership for a supreme effort :

Members should consider it a paramount duty to arouse British public opinion by every means in their power, in support of Republican Spain. Three things are essential : first, the supply of food (especially milk) not merely on a great, but a colossal scale : secondly, unremitting pressure on the National Government to compel it to go no farther on its shameful path : and thirdly, a constant winning over of more and more people in this country to the side of decency, by patiently and ceaselessly explaining to them the issues involved, and their own responsibility.

From now on, at all the Rallies, Spain was the principal topic. All the Club speakers, from whichever Party and from no Party, spoke on this theme; splendid collections were taken at them all for food and for medical aid.

In October, 1937, the Club also turned its attention to China. Ever since 1931 the long drawn-out "special undeclared war" of Japan against Chiang Kai-Shek's Chinese Republic had dragged on. The League of Nations refrained from invoking collective security or even condemning Japan.

There now appeared an entirely new factor in the situation. A Communist movement had long been established in China, and Chiang had made repeated and strenuous attempts to destroy it. In fact it was in this direction rather than against the Japanese that most of his efforts were directed. At last under the leadership of an unknown communist called Mao Tse Tung, the inhabitants of the communist areas in the interior gave up waiting for invasion, envelopment and extermination, or even the possibility of enduring an interminable seige. They packed what they could take with them, and set off on "the long march" of 6,000 miles to the north-west of China. This heroic adventure was described in the choice for October 1937, Edgar Snow's *Red Star Over China*. This book included the only existing biographical interview with Mao Tse Tung.

Snow's account of the long march was built up from the experiences of the men and women who took part in it, who marched and fought the whole of that 6,000 miles. We none of us knew that at the end of the Second World War it would be Mao and his peasant army which would drive Chiang Kai-Shek out of the country and set up the Communist Republic of China.

To understand the immensely complex situation in China, in

the autumn of 1937, demanded a good deal of solid background information which was provided in the *Left News* for October and November by two long articles by Professor Shelley Wang and H. D. Liem of the China Peace Committee. Snow's book became one of the most popular choices of the Club. It both made new members and strengthened the existing membership. Once again a tour of the country was organised. Groups in fifteen towns heard from Shelley Wang and Liem first hand accounts of the New China that was coming into being.

If one casts one's memory back to the rallies for Spain and the tour on China, one begins to grasp the immense range of the Club's activities. One also realises that it operated in depth and not merely in mass meetings. A great deal of the initiative in every field came from the groups and the members themselves. We provided the books and the speakers for the big meetings and tours and much else besides. They took the initiative in finding premises, organising film shows and dozens of other enterprises. We suggested, encouraged, helped, sent our area organisers around; but the will to learn, to do, to branch out in new ways, was already there.

CHAPTER V

THE TOWN THAT WAS MURDERED

IN RETROSPECT ONE tends to see the late thirties as the prelude to the war, and to see the whole period in terms of the menace of Nazi aggression. One forgets that fascism itself arose not simply as a particularly blatant form of chauvinism or German imperialism, but as a desperate attempt on the part of German capitalism to find a way out of the intolerable economic crisis which had engulfed not only Germany but the whole world. An explanation of the economic causes of fascism and imperialist war was expounded in several important Club volumes, notably Brailsford's *Why Capitalism Means War* and Strachey's *Coming Struggle for Power*.

The economic crisis grew steadily from the end of the first world war, and became increasingly acute in the years between 1933 and 1939, only mitigated to some degree by rearmament. Unemployment was still more than ten per cent in 1937. Over the whole post-war period from 1920 onwards, it seemed as if ten per cent of unemployment were the irreducible minimum. At the end of 1933 there were 3,000,000 unemployed; this number fell to 1,500,000 in the period immediately preceding the Second World War but it still meant appalling poverty for a vast number of people in this country. In the earlier period of the industrial crisis thousands of unemployed had marched to London from the Welsh coalfields, the Tyne shipbuilding towns and other places, to hold mass demonstrations of anger and bitter despair in the metropolis.

In spite of some economic advance, it was an inescapable fact that there still existed in Britain in the twenties a new "submerged tenth". Even outside the distressed areas, some ten per cent of the urban population was below the "poverty line" of the barest minimum subsistence. Moreover there appeared, side by side with "the poor", the "new poor", consisting of skilled workers made redundant by the closing of the pits, the collapse of the engineering and textile industries, and above all by the closing of the shipyards.

World trade fell by two-thirds at the worst period of the slump, and in the thirties in every port and estuary many ships of the mercantile marine were laid up, idle and rusting. The shipbuilding town of Jarrow had become derelict in the crisis, as though devastated by war. Its workers, led by their Member of Parliament, Ellen Wilkinson, had walked, ragged and ill shod, hungry and angry, from Tyneside to London. The Club choice —*The Town that was Murdered*—by taking Jarrow as a concrete example of what was happening in the North, brought home to its 40,000 readers the tragedy of economic crisis, and the consequent poverty and wretchedness.

It is strange how many people can be indifferent to human misery. Few are intelligent or sensitive enough to see the needs of others as vividly as they recognise their own. This we all realise when we look at the horrors of factory life in the early years of the nineteenth century, when children worked for fifteen hours a day in the cotton mills, and hours of labour for all, young and old, were limited only by the utmost capabilities of human endurance. These and other nameless iniquities will be found recorded in the impartial pages of blue-books and in such works as *The Town Labourer* by the Hammonds.[1] But from time to time there comes a new awareness of human pain, a new sense of responsibility. Great evils are at last seriously grappled with and suffering alleviated. The Club undoubtedly played its part in awakening the social conscience to the poverty of the thirties.

In the second month of the Club's existence G. C. M. McGonigle's *Poverty and Public Health* was announced. It was reviewed in the *Left News* for June 1936, and made the first "Additional book" in July. Published at 6s., it was made available to Club members, in a *blue* limp cover, for 2s. 6d.[2]

G. C. M. McGonigle was the Medical Officer of Health for Stockton-on-Tees, and his enquiries were statistical and carried out with complete objectivity and extreme care. No expert or

---

[1] Reprint of a Classic, for August, 1937.

[2] "Blue", good heavens! Never again did any Club volume appear except in the familiar *orange* covers, until the red board covers finally took their place—which was a pity. Vintage L.B.C. is in *orange* limp cloth binding.

critic subsequently ventured to challenge his findings. What he did was to compare incomes with the health and the death-rate of Stockton working-class families. There was a remarkable correlation between low wages and high death-rate. Families with an income between 25s. and 35s. a week died at a rate of 26 per 1,000. If the income was between 65s. and 75s. a week, the death-rate fell to 13 per 1,000. Sir John Boyd Orr, reviewing the book in the *Sunday Times*, wrote:

> The evidence suggests that two-thirds of our children are growing up under dietary conditions under which it is impossible to develop a normal, healthy adult. This may afford an explanation of the fact that of three men presenting themselves for recruitment, two have to be rejected as physically unfit.

McGonigle's book was the first of a series of books dealing with the problems of poverty and unemployment, and with the "distressed areas". The next, Wal Hannington's *The Problem of the Distressed Areas* (November 1937) was followed later by his *Ten Lean Years* (March 1940).

Hannington had been the Organiser of the National Unemployed Workers' Movement since the twenties, and I had met him when myself organising the unemployed at Gravesend and Tilbury in 1920. An engineer by trade, he was a man of great warmth of spirit and humour, of indomitable courage, and a skilful and ingenious leader of his men. He led the great Hunger Marches to London on many occasions and had been imprisoned six times. He also wrote another book dealing directly with this period—*Unemployed Struggles*.[3] Hannington brought home to the complacent and the well-disposed but unaware, the real tragedy caused by whole areas falling into decay—notably those concerned with coal, iron, steel and shipbuilding. In *The Distressed Areas* he dealt with the enquiries set on foot by the Special Areas Bill of 1934, and the eventual failure to find any answer to the problem. Hannington described the appalling conditions of these derelict areas: houses where 65 people had only two lavatories, the case of a single room inhabited by five people including a cripple with tuberculosis, to give but two examples of many. He brought home the real indignity of the *means test*, which cut down the dole in relation

[3] Lawrence & Wishart, 1936.

to any income from a householder's son or daughter who might be earning.

This exhaustive and objective study deeply stirred the conscience of the Club. It was an honest, substantial book, and it made the charitable and the complacent, and a good many politicians, very angry indeed.

Among other books published by the Club dealing with the working-class movement, this time from a different angle, was one by a Youth leader from Scotland called John Gollan—*Youth in British Industry*.[4] Gollan is now General Secretary to the British Communist Party.

One of our Club enthusiasts, Marjorie Chaplin, thought that it was not enough for Club members to read about these conditions. Most of them had no first-hand experience of what was happening in the distressed areas; wouldn't it be a good idea if they went and saw things for themselves? She proposed to take a team of Club members on a tour of one of the most hard hit districts, and she chose South Wales. There, with the help of a keen young miner, Cliff Wallace, they met unemployed groups, visited their homes, discussed the situation with Trade Union leaders, and came into first-hand contact with the facts behind Hannington's book. This was the first of such schools. The next covered four areas in South Wales: Merthyr, the Rhondda, Cardiff and Pontypridd. The programme of the schools included visits to the Unemployed Workers Clubs, to Trade Union Lodges, to collieries and factories, and also lectures on the economic history of South Wales, Unemployment Administration and so forth.

Two further schools were organised for the summer of 1938, one at Pontypridd and the other at Swansea. One of the most important consequences was the formation of a *Distressed Areas Group* which made itself responsible for these schools and brought many members from more privileged districts to meet the unemployed personally and to familiarise themselves with what such areas really looked like.

One of their activities was to work out the actual budgets of several families. We may perhaps give an example. They recorded the income and expenditure of a miner named O'Rourke with a wife and six children:

[4] An Additional book for August 1937.

Food for the week	£1 5s. 2d.
Rent, coal, light, clothing and tobacco	18s. 10d.
	£2 4s. 0d.

The whole family slept in two double beds. Prices were, of course, much lower than today, but wage rates in 1935, as stated by the Ministry of Labour, averaged 65s. a week in engineering, 69s. a week in cotton and 55s. in woollen manufacture.

The Merseyside Survey, made at this time, showed that nearly a third of the working-class population fell below the Rowntree Line.[5] A large proportion of the workers in cotton and coalmining fell below the generally accepted minimum standard.

A very important book issued by the Club in April 1937 was *The Condition of Britain* by G. D. H. Cole and his wife Margaret Cole. This was an exhaustive account of the condition of the working-class, covering the previous fifty years—statistical and factual and completely authoritative. Their conclusions on the condition of the unemployed were :

> That for a large section, especially in the depressed areas and industries and among the older workers, the existing conditions involve not only continuous mental suffering and deterioration, but also bodily privation by which the coming generation is bound to be gravely damaged both in stamina and physique.

The reaction of the Trade Union Movement and British Labour was brilliantly recorded in Allen Hutt's *Post-War History of the British Working Class* (June 1937), one of the most important books on social history published by the Club.

London itself was not without its own problem of poverty. The Stepney Group, working in conjunction with the City of London Group and the Central London Area Committee, launched their own enquiry into conditions in the East End. They organised conducted tours in districts which before the war, in many parts, looked like a distressed area, and in localities

[5] Seebohm Rowntree, in his book *The Human Needs of Labour* (Longmans Green, 1937) attempted to establish a minimum standard of living based on the nutritional requirements laid down by the British Medical Association.

hardest hit by unemployment. The plan followed was to arrange a number of itineraries for small groups to follow each under the leadership of a Club member who knew the district and its problems.

In the years that followed, the Club regularly returned to various aspects of the social problem, with both factual studies such as Wal Hannington's *Ten Lean Years: An Examination of the Record of the National Government in the Field of Unemployment,* the choice for March 1940, and Charles Segal's enquiry into the social conditions associated with backward children, *Penn'orth of Chips,* an Additional book for May 1939, and with theoretical studies such as G. D. H. Cole's *The Means to Full Employment* and *National Capitalism* by Ernest Davies, the Additional book for August 1939. Davies' book was reviewed at some length by John Strachey. Its theme was the irresistible development of the great monopolies—in the steel industry for instance—and the inter-twining of the state with the great combines. The author was able to show that the destruction of Jarrow was due not only to the decline of ship-building but to the strangling, by the great steel monopolies, of the project to give Jarrow a steel works. The steady disintegration of the South Wales coalfield was seen to be largely the result of the creation of a ring of monopolies in the coal industry.

The tragedy of the derelict mining industry of South Wales was the theme of a moving autobiographical account of the life of a Welsh miner, B. L. Coombes, whose book *These Poor Hands* was published by the Club at the same time as *National Capitalism.* Thus the Club focused its theoretical analysis of the economic problems concerning the mines on the personal experience of a man who had endured all the harrowing experiences of a miner in those days of unemployment and crisis—victimisation, over-work when in the mine, accidents, the dust-choked lungs of a silicosis victim, and all the rest. Such a book admirably supplemented the theoretical studies of Strachey and Davies. It gave Club members a living portrait of life as it was then lived in the distressed areas of what was still the richest country in Europe.[6]

[6] We should not console ourselves with the delusion that in 1970 we live in an affluent society in which poverty has virtually disappeared. Even in the U.S.A. three successive presidents have launched their campaigns against poverty, and have been compelled to call them off owing to financial

Strachey followed the *Theory and Practice of Socialism* with *What are we to Do?* (March 1938), a lucid exposition of Lenin's theory of the Party, but in neither book were many pages devoted to the question of the transition from capitalism to socialism. Then in *A Programme for Progress* (January 1940), the argument was resumed, and with a sense of shock his socialist disciples witnessed a remarkable feat of rapid back pedalling. For what was proposed was nothing less than an ingenious plan to get capitalism working again, by a reform of the monetary mechanism. We were really back to the Strachey of 1930. At that time Oswald Mosley had been a Minister in the Labour Government and Strachey had been his Parliamentary Private Secretary. Strachey and Mosley had worked out a monetary solution of the economic crisis, which was subsequently adopted as part of the programme of Mosley's New Party which Strachey joined, but almost immediately afterwards left.

Something very like this monetary theory now reappeared in Strachey's *Programme for Progress*. It was the subject of his lecture course at the last Summer School of the Club at Digswell Park in 1939. In his *Capitalist Crisis* he had examined and rejected these monetary panaceas—but what was this but another one! After the War there appeared a further essay, *Contemporary Capitalism*—which was a programme for Britain based on the recognition (absent from his earlier books) of the effectiveness of democratic pressure in modifying, if not preventing, the worsening of conditions under capitalism which Marxists had predicted.

---

difficulties; in England a quarter of a million children in large families are below the poverty line; the housing situation appears irremediable. Peter Townsend, in the journal of the Child Poverty Action Group, says "We are all concerned about widespread poverty and squalor, about large sections of the population left behind in the advance towards prosperity." (*Poverty,* January 1970.)

CHAPTER VI

THE THIRD YEAR OF THE CLUB
1938–1939

THE RAPID DEVELOPMENT of the Club demanded an equally rapid increase in the personnel at Henrietta Street. Gollancz, however, was still responsible for the normal publishing activity of his firm, as well as the Left Book Club to which he devoted every spare moment. New staff were taken on by the business department to cope with the flood of applications for membership, and with the *PLEASE* leaflets, signed at meetings, asking for particulars of the Club. Then there were the book-sellers to be informed and negotiated with; and the inevitable resignations, which are a feature of all organisations. V.G.'s considerable personal correspondence was conducted not only on the difficult questions of Club policy which constantly arose, and on the coming choices, but also with individual members who wrote to him on every conceivable topic. (A good many of these letters were passed on to me, especially the many letters we received on religious questions. I was thought qualified to deal with these on the basis of some twenty years' experience as a Presbyterian Minister as well as being during all these years a socialist.) Added to all this, the selection, actual production, and usual technical and business arrangements, without which no books can be published, had to be made, not only for the choice of the month, but for the four or five extra Club books which were selected, printed and published every month. All this was supervised by V.G. who left nothing entirely to other people.

V.G. was also the speaker at four or five rallies each week when the successive campaigns were running. From as far away as Nottingham or Plymouth he would be driven back to London after the meeting, arriving home in the small hours, snatching an hour or two's sleep, rapidly scanning the morning papers and appearing at the office at 8.30 a.m. However busy he was he always took the carbon copies of our letters home with him and they were in our trays at 9 a.m. next morning with his pencilled comments. At about 11, except when he was extraordinarily busy, one went down for a daily conference on the letters, including anything urgent in the day's post or concerning the immediate problem—jobs, the rallies, tours or group possibilities of the moment.

It was an exacting job that was enjoyable because of the intensity, the pace and the thoroughness with which everything was done, and above all because of the zest with which V.G. would leap at a new possibility, seize on your suggestions if he liked them, or compel you to explore some new idea of his own. Thus it was that within one year of launching the Club we were already engaged in a dozen major projects that no-one had dreamed of when we started.

The organisational apparatus which set the wheels moving, supplied the speakers, organised the tours, and lectures and meetings was the rapidly growing *Groups Department*. This moved in a short while to its own offices at 17-18 Henrietta Street, where it occupied the whole of the third floor. As the groups multiplied so did the staff until it consisted of four district organisers, Sheila Lynd for London, George Thomas for Wales and the South-West, Jane Conway for the Midlands and South-East, John Burns for the North. The office of the Groups Department was in the charge of Betty Reid. Later the Theatre Guild was added to our many responsibilities.

The groups were in close touch both with V.G. and myself. The correspondence was enormous, we offered advice, and dealt with their difficulties.

Those of us whose main responsibility was that of organising the groups found that we were getting to know our people; there was a close personal relationship between us all. V.G. communicated his own urgency and passionate concern through his warm and interested contacts with members and conveners. Our letters were never merely business or organisational ones. We knew and were intimately concerned with the hopes, the experiences, the new ventures of our members and the groups.

We planned the work of the district organisers on the basis of visits of about six weeks' duration to their areas to see the groups, organise tours and lectures by special speakers, to form new groups, to investigate what was being done in various fields, to make suggestions for improvements and new ventures and then to return and report.

Another big job was to commence the preparations for the rallies and then to supervise the work for them. These were always under our control, because we wanted no mistakes, no shortcomings in their preparation. Any carelessness or neglect would mean something less than a full house and that we usually avoided. It made an enormous difference to a meeting if the hall was literally packed—not a seat vacant. If we charged for admission, as we usually had to do to cover the expenses, we always added to the posters and tickets, "Some free seats at the door", to make sure that any seats not sold were filled. We advised on the typography of leaflets and posters, V.G. being exceptionally gifted in effective lay-out and printing. We saw to it that the publicity was good, that the tickets were being pushed, that local civic personalities, trade unionists, clergy, headmasters and university men (rarer in those days than now) were invited to be on the platform; that every likely organisation was canvassed for its support. Rallies didn't just happen. The response was waiting to be aroused. We had the message. But that response had to be stimulated by energetic work—and people had to be told that there really was something worth coming to hear. We got to know a large number of keen individuals. We heard their enthusiastic reports, or confessions of failure. We helped them grapple with difficulties. We made on-the-spot suggestions for new ventures, put them in touch with other groups, gave them encouragement and every kind of help in our power.

Whatever task the Club turned its hand to, it never lost sight of its primary aim, the endeavour to *comprehend* the situation. It demanded, and sought to give *understanding*. When he asked himself, said V.G., what little he could do, the answer was, "You can help to enlighten people. You can show them that, if capitalism persists, this sort of crisis is inevitable, and the final result will be war." That was his faith.

In the international field it was a different problem. It was a question of preventing war that seemed just round the corner : the terrible danger posed by the Nazi domination of Europe, not only of the Balkans and Poland, but of France and Britain. "Our very salvation," said V.G., "depends on the political education of the masses." In January 1939, he urged the Club to make the year one of supreme effort. "The primary task of the Left Book Club during 1939 is to see to it that at some point during that year, and at as early a point as possible, the tide of public opinion becomes so strong that it bursts the dams and carries all before it.[1]

We have already given a picture of the groups as they developed in the first year of the Club's existence. The third year saw a further advance. The organisers were now in the field. We helped the growth of the groups by supplying them with lists of Club members in their areas. We placed recruiting leaflets in every copy of the monthly choice and asked our members to pass these on to friends. At all our meetings we had leaflets ready for distribution. We went to meetings of other organisations and placed our leaflets on all the seats before proceedings began, or distributed them to people entering and leaving. In one month 140,000 yellow recruiting leaflets went out to members, and 86,500 to booksellers. V.G. constantly stressed the urgency of the Club's mission, and the rapidly decreasing time in which it could be achieved.

When a special recruiting campaign was launched the groups were urged to send delegates to local Labour Parties, trade unions, Cooperative Societies, and other progressive organisations to explain the Club. The groups went in for selective canvassing of doctors, teachers and clergymen. Stunts were sometimes organised. For instance, the Hastings Group as a special recruiting effort, organised a procession of fifteen cars, displaying Left Book Club posters and streamers, to an open air meeting on the sea front, at which a collection was taken for Spanish Aid.

The groups now began to set up Area Federations. These appeared in Birmingham, Manchester, W. London, S.W. London, Croydon (Surrey), Merseyside, Durham, Hull, Nottingham and many other places. The Federations often produced monthly bulletins giving information about all the activities of the various associated groups, with particulars of combined meetings.

In 1939 we issued a *Group Handbook* of 64 pages giving practical, detailed advice on running the groups with suggestions based on two years' experience. There were hints and warnings,

[1] *Left News* (January 1939).

tips on publicity, ideas for week-end schools, instructions on how to run rallies.

We were now able to make full use of two film organisations, Kino, and The Film and Photo League. Kino offered a number of Russian, anti-fascist and Spanish films. In addition to *The Defence of Madrid*, they included *China Strikes Back*, and two films by Ivor Montagu, *Behind the Spanish Lines*, and *Spanish A.B.C.* The Film and Photo League made short documentaries, and hired them out, or showed them for a few shillings. Some of these were moving and realistic sequences depicting social conditions here in England at the time. Among these were *Winter*, about cold weather and the poor, *Bread, Hunger March 1936* and *Dock Workers*. The Kino full-length films were money spinners. Cambridge ran *Spanish Earth* for a week and raised £1,000 for the Left Book Club food-ship for Spain. We urged all the groups to use films in these ways, "to mobilise the hitherto disorganised but vaguely progressive feeling which is at present without a voice in the land. Films provide an excellent means of gathering into our groups the progressive-minded people of your district."[2]

To make this picture convincing, and give some concrete examples of the work during this year, one must particularise. Consider a small, rather remote Cathedral town like Ely, where there was practically no political activity or intellectual life. Here the economist and statistician Professor Jurgen Kuczynski, who was on a lecture tour to introduce his Club book, *The Condition of the Workers in Great Britain, Germany and the Soviet Union* (in the course of which he visited twenty groups), held an extraordinarily successful meeting. The convener reported :

> The whole group is delighted with our first public meeting. We attribute the excellent attendance to personal canvassing. We received congratulations afterwards from many prominent Conservatives. I have never seen our members so excited. Groups were standing outside the hall long after the meeting.[3]

Woking, in Surrey, was another quiet semi-rural town where the Club was doing remarkable work. Starting in April 1937

[2] *Left News* (March 1939).
[3] *Left News* (July 1939).

with a meeting of ten, they canvassed trade unions and other societies, sent a delegate to L.B.C. Theatre Guild Conference, and organised a film meeting on Spain to which 250 people came. Woking Labour Party offered to arrange joint activities. Discussion meetings proceeded regularly. Wal Hannington spoke on "The Distressed Areas" at a public meeting at which the Theatre Group put on a play about conditions in the distressed areas. There was an attendance of over 200 people at this meeting. A one-day school followed with an attendance of 60. The proceedings for the year terminated with a Christmas party at a member's house.

An excellent example of quiet steady educational work, combined with public meetings, so that the group steadily enlarged and its work extended.

Stepney was always a lively group. In January 1938 it reported running a series of educational classes in Economics, Politics and Modern Languages in connection with the Quaker Social Institute. In addition they had a Gramophone Recital Course, while the Dramatic Section again worked in close cooperation with the Quakers. The monthly meetings took the form of open lectures followed by discussion and the speakers included Sir Walter Layton, Wal Hannington, Dr Norman Hare, John Strachey and Professor Marrack. Attendance was usually well over a hundred. The group also launched out with P.T. classes and a Swimming Club.

There was a vigorous group in Bradford whose programme was recorded in the *Left News* for September 1937 as an example of advance planning. The completed series of meetings and other events ran as follows:

Sept. 5   Discussion on *The People's Front* opened by representatives of the Labour and Liberal Parties.
Sept. 19   The Rev. Nicholson Palmer on *Towards the Christian Revolution*.
Oct. 1   Social and Dramatic performance.
Oct. 3   Herr Graupner on *The Spirit and Structure of German Fascism*.
Oct. 10   Joint meeting with the W.E.A. Lecture by the Tutor on *A Philosophy for Modern Man*.
Oct. 30   Rally.
Nov. 5   Debate with Catholics: Strachey v. Papal Encyclicals.
Nov. 10   Performance of Clifford Odets' *Waiting for Lefty*.

Nov. 21   Joint meeting with Coop. and L.P. Speaker Cecil
          Jones, M.P. on *The Labour Party in Perspective*.
Dec.   5 Wal Hannington on *The Distressed Areas*.

A typical small suburban group with no star speakers but
lucky enough to get a distinguished lecturer for one of its regular
courses was Tulse Hill in South London. It had a steady membership of 40. Its general aim was to have one book talk and
discussion and one topical meeting every month. The group
initiated the local Basque Children's Committee, organised
regular social gatherings in the winter and rambles in the
summer; ran a public meeting in Lambeth Town Hall with
an attendance of over 500; played an energetic part in the
distribution of the Club leaflets on Spain and Czechoslovakia;
organised theatre parties to see plays of social significance; and
ran a series of eight lectures on Social Philosophy by Randall
Swingler with an average attendance of 40, covering such
questions as "Man's Place in Nature", "Philosophy, Religion
and Utopia", "Principles of Organisation and Action in Politics".

Central London ran courses in the Russian language by Dr
Falchikov; Coventry organised week-end camps on the river-
side at Banton; Swindon published a monthly called *North
Wilts Viewpoint*. Mansfield organised a Conference on "Religion
and Socialism" with the Bishop in the Chair, the speaker being
the well-known Anglo-Catholic Dr E. L. Mascall. For London
members I gave a series of lectures on "The History of
Philosophy" in Marx House with an attendance of over 50.

An idea mooted in the summer of 1939 was to hold seaside
rallies to bring together Club members on holiday and other
visitors as well. Groups organised rambles, garden parties, day-
schools, and one group, Southport, "a Midsummer Rally with
a wide variety of activities—a play by the Theatre Group,
rambles, games, dancing on the lawn, yarns from Spain by an
International Brigader and a tea fit for democrats."

One of the most ambitious projects of Victor Gollancz, once
he had got the Club really moving, was to launch a weekly
socialist or Popular Front paper, to be called *The Left News
Weekly*, on the basis of his 40,000 members. The idea was first
mooted in February 1937. The *Left News*, at first quite a small
affair, was growing every month, from 15 pages it had expanded
to 30 pages in six months and it was to jump once again to 40

pages by September 1938. But as it only appeared once a month there was no way in which some immediate crisis could be dealt with and the Club called to action. What V.G. wanted, above all things, was a *weekly* opportunity of dealing with rapidly changing events, both as to providing information, giving an immediate lead and, as he rightly saw, translating comprehension into instant action.

Another good reason for launching a weekly was that V.G. had discovered a much larger "Left" public than had been suspected; and realising that it had flocked into the Club because it was eager for really full and detailed information, would it not also be ready for a paper? Finally, although the *Left News* always contained very meaty and highly relevant articles, and factual information pieces, it had to leave out far more than it could print.

V.G. envisaged the paper as consisting of about seven articles —two of about 7,000 words, two of 4,000, one of 3,000 and two of 2,000. It would be thoroughly informative and factual. Each issue he hoped would be unique, and not "just another paper". He began to make plans for tapping special sources of information in France and in the Fascist countries. And he inserted a post card in the *Left News* for February, to get the views of members.

In the next number (March 1937), he came back with his verdict from the Club members. Seventy-five per cent wanted it. V.G. began to organise. He engaged Vincent Duncan-Jones as a possible editor, and in any case to help him take the first practical steps. He proposed, of course, to use the Club and particularly the groups, of which there were now 40, as publicity centres for getting new readers, while the Club itself, he hoped, would guarantee from the first a circulation of 20,000 or more.

It may seem surprising that nothing more was heard of the Weekly until September 1938, though many members wrote in asking when it was going to start. V.G. then announced that the scheme was off. A new Left-wing paper, the *Tribune*, had come into being, under the auspices of a board consisting of Cripps, Laski, Aneurin Bevan, G. R. Strauss, M.P., Ellen Wilkinson and William Mellor. He himself was going to join the board. He had negotiated an agreement whereby every week there would be so many pages for the Club, edited by V.G., and written for the Club—a twenty-four page paper would have four pages under the control of the Club, a larger paper even more.

V.G. then worked out one of his rather complicated and ingenious special forms of membership—"Tribune Membership". Any regular subscriber to the paper could become a member of the Club if he promised to take at least two Club books in each year at 3s. 6d. He could also order any of the optional books.

Here was a drawing together of the Left Book Club and the weekly journal of a really militant section of the Labour Party. As V.G. wrote :

> When such a combination of forces takes place, the effect is infinitely greater than that of simple addition, rather does it mean that an altogether new stage has been reached in the mobilisation of progressive people against war, against fascism, for liberty, and for a higher standard of life, and that the forces which have for so long fought, however bravely a series of rearguard actions, may now go forward to conquer, as they must conquer, the heights.[4]

In addition to the books already mentioned there were many others of considerable importance. Whatever the Club turned its hand to it never forgot that the essence of its work was educational.

In August 1937 had come a "Reprint" of *The Town Labourer* by the Hammonds, a well known account of the conditions of the workers between 1760 and 1832, and this had been followed by Dorothy Macardle's very big book, *The Irish Republic* (a "Supplementary").

In 1938 came a book on *The Juvenile Labour Market* by Jewkes, and two important books on the working of our legal system, W. H. Thompson's *Civil Liberties* (Thompson was a well known lawyer concerned with the Trade Union Movement), and *Justice in England* by "A Barrister", who was Miss Mavis Hill of the Inner Temple. This book, which was the choice for July 1938, questioned certain assumptions of our legal system. Our judges, "Barrister" declared, are incorruptible, but the very structure of our legal system protects the *status quo* against radical change. "In an unequal society like ours the

[4] *Left News* (September 1938).

legal system is bound to promote injustice. For it makes justice very largely a matter of wealth; and it makes the doctrines of which the Courts dispose principles built upon a presumed identity between the power of the privileged class and the welfare of the State."

An important book on the Agricultural situation was Lord Addison's *A Policy for British Agriculture,* the choice for January 1939. Addison had in mind the possibility of greatly increasing our home grown food supplies, and at the same time improving the very bad conditions and wages of the agricultural labourers. His first proposal was to nationalise all agricultural land, which was then to be controlled by a "National Agricultural Commission" under the Minister of Agriculture. He proposed to regularise prices by a marketing scheme for all the principal products of farming, making one market of the whole country to avoid regional gluts. One of his aims was to deal with the considerable waste of present distribution methods, and the very greatly enhanced prices of food entirely owing to the payments made to middlemen, to the disadvantage of farmer and consumer alike.

Turning for a moment to international affairs, the fundamental issues raised by the earlier books on Nazi Germany and later on China were illuminated by some first hand records of the actual situation in these countries. In February 1938 the Club published *Our Street*, a chronicle written in the heart of Fascist Germany by Jan Petersen, as a Supplementary book. The chronicle took the form of a novel under the Nazis in one street, written in Germany and smuggled out baked inside two chocolate cakes. It was a most moving account of what life for ordinary people was like. Sylvia Townsend Warner said of it in the *Left News* for January 1938, "However strongly entrenched Nazidom may be, this book of Petersen's condemns it as a falsity, as a failure, as something alien to the people, and realised by them as both brutal and ridiculous."

China Fights Back by Agnes Smedley was the choice for December 1938. It took up the story of the great march by Edgar Snow almost exactly from the point where Snow left it, at the outbreak of China's open war with Japan, and reported on the first great retreat of the Japanese forces. This marked the emergence on to the field of history of Mao Tse Tung. Agnes Smedley's book was splendid reportage and her first-hand picture of the advance regiments of the old Red Army from Kiangsi marching to battle is breath taking. How did Miss Smedley know all about this? She was there.

One or two books of a different order must be mentioned to make clear once more that the Club was not by any means entirely concerned with international politics. The first attempt to relate the teachings of Marx and Freud has already been mentioned. It was published quite early in the Club's history. Another and perhaps more professional treatment was to be found in *Sigmund Freud,* the Additional book for September 1968, by Francis Bartlett. Far more critical than Reuben Osborn in the earlier book, Bartlett nevertheless argued that Freud was a genuine scientific worker who had discovered new truths in regard to the conditions of the human mind. Osborn, however, reappeared in a highly controversial book on *The Psychology of Reaction,* the Additional book for April 1938. It was first a revealing analysis of the psychological basis of fascism and its methods of propaganda, designed to show "how man's unconscious emotional impulses, stimulated by irrational and menacing economic conditions, can be exploited by the fascists for reactionary purposes." He then dealt with some of the psychological aspects of Anti-Semitism; and in the concluding chapters dealt critically with the ultra-revolutionary romanticism of Trotsky, so vigorously denounced by Lenin.

The ultra-Leftist philosophy again appeared in a scholarly book on the French revolutionary *Blanqui* by Neil Stewart, the Additional book for June 1939. Marxism is sometimes supposed to favour an essentially "putsch" type of insurrection carried out by a conspiratorial minority. This was indeed the view of Blanqui who practised this kind of uprising and spent thirty seven years of his life in prison as a result. His theories were strongly opposed by both Marx and Lenin, who saw no possibility of radical social change without the informed and conscious participation of the masses. Neil Stewart argues that "the phantasy of overturning an entire society through the action of a small conspiracy" is a dangerous delusion.

In August 1940 Leo Huberman, who had written one of the Club's most popular books on economic history, *Man's Worldly Goods,* once again scored a success with *We, The People,* a clear and readable account of the beginnings and development of the American nation.

In June 1938 there appeared Joseph Freeman's *American Testament*. The autobiography of a poet and writer, it was concerned with the awakening of a whole generation of young American intellectuals between 1920 and the rise of Hitler in the thirties, and the impact upon them of the Russian Revolution; among his friends and close associates John Dos Passos, Max Eastman, Sherwood Anderson, Mike Gold, Floyd Bell, Scott Nearing (still writing for the *Monthly Review*) and John Reed whose book *Ten Days that shook the World* was a first-hand account of the Russian Revolution. Reed is buried beneath the wall of the Kremlin.

Laski called Freeman's book one that "the historian will want to quote as an index to some of the most significant features of those momentous years" (*Left News*, June 1938). Its theme was the earnest desire of intellectuals to serve the people's movement in their own fields. Many of them, Freeman records, spoke of "a sense of identity of their efforts towards a great literature and a great poetry for America with the struggle of the working class for emancipation and reform."

Freeman worked in Russia for some years as a translator and met the poet Mayakowski and the film producer Eisenstein. Some of the most interesting chapters in the book record his friendship and discussion with them.

As a translator he was present at the great political discussion in which opponents of the policy of building socialism in one country argued their case in Party congresses and public meetings, including Trotsky, Zinoviev, Kamenev and Bukharin. One of the interesting facts which emerges from this book is the entirely different atmosphere, the greater informality, the much greater scope for free and vigorous discussion in Russia in these early years compared with the later period of the Trials.

It was not only in Britain that members of the Left Book Club were found. They joined from all over the world—from wherever obstacles were not placed against obtaining the books as was the case in India and the United States—but we had many readers in those countries notwithstanding.

Very early in the life of the Club, groups began to appear abroad, and by the beginning of 1937 they were to be found in Paris, Brussels, Zurich, and farther afield in Colombo, the Gold

Coast, Auckland and South Africa. Later they appeared in many other countries.

Among the South African Groups, Johannesburg deserves special mention. Many distinguished scholars were among this group's lecturers, including Judge Krause, Professor Hoernlé, Professor La Fouche, Professor Grey, Dr Murray and Dr Sachs. There were also lively groups in Cape Town, Bulawayo, Salisbury and Pretoria, and a small group of six or seven people 200 miles from Pretoria at Waterfall Boven. Elsewhere in Africa Groups quickly appeared—in Accra, Freetown and Sierra Leone, and there were Club members in Uganda and Kenya.

Australia soon had a most vigorous Left Book Club movement. By the end of 1938 there were fourteen groups round Melbourne. The Victorian membership reached 1,500, and here they organised a Research Group to publish pamphlets and books on social conditions in Australia. New South Wales had 1,500 members and 30 groups.

The Australian Government was very alarmed at that time about what it regarded as subversive activities. One of the Perth members of the Club, a pharmaceutical chemist, was interrogated by plain-clothes political police, who proceeded to examine his books. The first was Melville's *Moby Dick*. "Who was Moby Dick?" "A whale!" This remark appeared sheer contempt for the operations of the law. Then they found the Dean of Canterbury's book on Russia, but were discomposed to find the author a high ecclesiastic. Finally there was Attlee's *Labour Party in Perspective*. This appeared to them damning evidence of criminal intent. Away they went with it threatening the direst consequences. However, these never followed. Australia published its own *Left News* to supplement the London edition.

In New Zealand there were 23 Groups by the summer of 1939, when a National Left Book Club Conference was held.

The Club appeared in Canada and groups were formed in Ontario, Toronto, Kingston, Winnipeg, Victoria and Edmonton. There were ten groups in Toronto.

In November 1938 we were informed that as a direct result of the influence of the Left Book Club a similar organisation had been set on foot for Sweden, Finland, Norway, Iceland and Denmark. The organisers planned to publish four books a year and a periodical *Nord-Europa* in two editions, one in Swedish for Sweden and Finland, and one in Norwegian and Danish for the other three countries.

Left Book Groups also existed in Sweden, Switzerland, Egypt, Jerusalem and Haifa. A group of 30 met in Kingston, Jamaica.

These overseas Groups were in constant communication with us. No small part of my time was devoted to establishing very close personal relations by correspondence. All sorts of organisational problems were put to us, and the results of their discussions were sent for our comments and for light on difficult problems.

In the United States the books could only reach individuals who obtained them indirectly by getting a friend in England to buy them. This was because, owing to copyright law, many of the books could not be sold in the United States in the English edition. But there was great interest in the Club and at least one group met and discussed the books in Cambridge, Massachusetts. Harold Laski, who was a frequent visitor to the United States, and lectured from time to time in several universities, wrote that wherever he went he found people who had read the books. And in half a score of widely separated places he came across groups of men and women who met regularly to discuss them.

It was difficult to get Club books into India. The *Left News* was put on the prohibited list by the Indian censorship; the books were frequently confiscated by the Customs. In spite of these difficulties the Club had many readers in India, and various devices were resorted to to get the books and the *Left News* past the official barriers. The high level of political consciousness among Indian intellectuals, and also the influence of Nehru, who was friendly towards the Club, meant that the books were eagerly read and appreciated.

The Club at home in England developed a strong interest in India. On July 6th, 1938, a large public meeting at the Queen's Hall, under the auspices of the Club, was addressed by Nehru. The choice for May, 1940, was R. Palme Dutt's *India To-day*, a vigorous onslaught on British rule, and a herald of the independence which India achieved after the War.

CHAPTER VII

CLUB ACTIVITIES

BY THE TIME the Club was properly established, the hopes of the founders had materialised in a readership of 50,000, organised in 900 groups. Going beyond the monthly choice, the Club was pouring out Additional, Supplementary, Topical and Educational books in large numbers. But although this was totally unexpected and abundantly welcome, it was the vigorous life of the Club, as it expressed itself not only in the groups but in other ways that was even more surprising. Though the initiative and the breakthrough into new activities came from the members of the groups as often as from the centre, Victor Gollancz was exceptionally quick to recognise new ideas, to welcome them, publicise them, and put the weight of the Club and the *Left News* behind them. There was a reciprocal inter-action between leaders and the living Club.

Two new forms of Club activity were emerging. First, the big political thrust of the rallies, which drew larger audiences than any one political party could obtain at that time. Yet these were not party meetings, for members of all parties and representatives of all shades of progressive thought sat on the platforms. Nothing like this had been anticipated when the Club was founded.

Second, there sprang up a great variety of cultural and intellectual movements, associated with the Club, within the Arts and professions. They were not initiated by us. They appeared because the Club had stimulated everywhere a new consciousness of the times, its perils, its opportunities, its chal-lenge. People previously not concerned with anything beyond their work, were disturbed, excited, eager to learn, to talk and argue, to join with others in enquiry, to find what should be done. There was abroad a new and forward-reaching spirit of unrest. The Club itself was the expression of this, and became the catalyst which set other minds moving.

Here is a passage from one of the many letters we received,

on this occasion from someone who declared that they had hitherto been conservative in their general attitude :

The horror of our times is certainly a challenge to every single person, if only one can find a way to answer the challenge —even in the smallest degree. I take it the L.B.C. is to help the perplexed to clear their minds and to get at the facts, as well as to offer the willing an opportunity for work, and as one of the disillusioned and perplexed I would like to thank you.

Now as these groupings sprang up, they met with an instant and unexpected response. It was remarkable, for example, how the actors suddenly became interested in Spain, in peace, in the crises of the time; and the doctors, and scientists; and groups of workers in factories and railway stations; teachers, scientists, school-girls, tramway-men, musicians. The *Left News* reported these beginnings, and at once fresh people came along to form the groups. Even more was done by individuals communicating their own interest and new attitudes to colleagues and friends.

There was concern, eagerness to know, to find out, to explore new ideas, to experiment, to unite for effective action. It was the spirit of the times. It gave birth to the Club, it was fostered and spread by the Club; but it had many other sources and forms of expression in those difficult and confusing days.

If anyone had the idea that the Club was mainly a book producing affair, or only an organisation concerned with pro- paganda for Collective Security and Peace, it could be shown how, as a direct consequence of the books and the meetings, the lectures and the *Left News,* which began to carry many pages of news about the ever widening circle of Club activities, there came into being that considerable range of organisations and groupings among those concerned with the arts and the professions that we have just mentioned.

The well known literary personalities who formed the Readers and Writers Group, insisted that it should be a *readers'* as well as a writers' group because they felt that the appreciative and critical *reader* was inseparable from the writer. The Conway Hall was completely filled for its open meeting on "Literature and the People", with Victor Gollancz in the chair. Among those who spoke were Richard Church, Rose Macaulay, Rex

Warner, Olaf Stapledon, Norman Collins, and Elmer Rice the American dramatist.

Regular meetings were held in the top room of the Roseberry Hotel in Newport Street, and few progressive writers of the time did not appear there. Langston Hughes, the Negro poet, read his poems, Rex Warner opened a discussion on his novel *The Wild Goose Chase*. Arthur Calder Marshall, Edgell Rickword, Alick West, Randall Swingler, the young Indian novelist Mulk Raj Anand, were all associated with the group. Pamela Hansford Johnson, who spoke on "Women, Literature, and the Left", introduced the Left Book Club into her novel *The Monument*.

Maurice Richardson, now of the *Observer,* opened a discussion on Ralph Fox's *Novel and the People* and sectional discussions were organised on Jane Austen and D. H. Lawrence. It will be seen that the activities of the Readers and Writers Group went far beyond the political preoccupations of the time; but of course all those who participated in these discussions also showed sympathy with the Club's stand on Spain and peace and the struggle against fascism.

When the London Writers, including the Club members, but very many more, signed their protest against Franco's subjection of Spain, T. S. Eliot was the only well-known name not found on the list. Auden wrote at that time his own well-known poem on Spain.

The *poets* themselves formed a separate group, mainly with the aim of venturing into new verse, and encouraging poetic creation. They published an interesting little journal *Poetry for the People*. One rare copy contains original work by twenty-five contributors including some unknown poets and some as well-known as Randall Swingler, Edgell Rickword, Alec Craig, Geoffrey Parsons and John Manifold.

They trained their members to recite poetry at meetings of the groups, Co-operative Guilds, League of Nations and Trade Unions. They began the production of illustrated broadsheets, thus reviving a very vigorous use of poetry. These were sold in such places as the Caledonian Market, and outside factories. They declared that they were "trying to restore the traditional link between poetry and the people, going out to the people and letting them hear poetry that had some connection with reality and their daily lives, poetry which by its clarity and compactness of expression stabs like a searchlight into the confusion and contradiction of our experience."

Poetry and the People was enlarged and broadened in its scope to become *Our Time,* which had a freshness and quality of its own. Its editors were Beatrix Lehmann, Ben Frankel, the composer, and Randall Swingler. It launched into criticism of music, books, the theatre and writing, as well as continuing to publish poems, stories and reportage. In its programme the editors declared that "It will fight any tendency to regard art in any form as an escape. It will insist that only culture which aims at revitalising the human spirit in the days of its greatest test will be accepted as valid." The Poets Group eventually produced an anthology, *Poems of Freedom,* with an introduction by W. H. Auden. The editor was John Mulgan.

The London Poets' Group reported in the *Left News* that their members had heard lectures from Louis MacNeice, Charles Madge, Montagu Slater and Cecil Day Lewis. Day Lewis also spoke at a rally at Glastonbury, taking as his subject "Fascism and Literature". He said that

among those who had taken up arms against fascism were a great company of writers whose hearts had gone out towards Democracy and Social advance. We English writers are following in the traditions of those great Englishmen, Shakespeare, Milton, Blake, Shelley and Byron, for freedom is the first condition of the human soul.

In the conflict with fascism, he said, the Left Book Club was doing a great deal. He strongly approved of bringing the realities of the situation to the attention of the people through plays and poetry.

Turning to the groups associated with the Theatre, there were the *professional actors,* which we have mentioned before, and then there were the *amateur theatrical groups.* The professionals had a mailing list of 300 members and sympathisers. Many well known names were closely associated with the group —one recalls Michael Redgrave, Sybil Thorndike, Lewis Casson, Beatrix Lehmann, Miles Malleson, Van Gyseghem and Gerald Savory. The days when actors, along with musicians and artists, considered that politics were nothing to do with art and the drama were no more. The *Left News* records meetings of the Professional Group on "The Distressed Areas"; "The Condition of the English Theatre"; "The Left Theatre in England"; and on each of the Club choices as they were issued. The aim was to alternate the book of the month with some special topics connected with the drama and its professional problems.

The Amateurs were organised in the Left Book Club Theatre Guild under John Allen and later Paul Eisler—already mentioned under the cultural work of the Club.

Whatever other activities were going on—rallies, plays, Summer Schools, public lectures—the steady *educational work of the Club* continued and was the real basis of its influence.

The intense interest of the Club at first in Spain and later in China and Russia, its deep concern for poverty in England, sometimes gave the impression that it was becoming almost entirely a political organisation. This was never true. The public meetings, when we began to organise them to follow up the Albert Hall Rallies, certainly showed that the country was deeply concerned with these political issues, and that the Club was the most vigorous and active of all the organisations striving to awaken public opinion; but if one considered any particular district, there would be only one L.B.C. rally in the course of the year, and for the rest of that period, the Club would be steadily carrying on its lectures, discussions, filmshows, plays and week-end schools. And the flow of the books was preponderantly educational.

In this work an important part was played by the *Educational series*, which consisted of short introductions to a broad range of subjects at the low price of sixpence to Club members and one shilling to the public (1s. 6d. clothbound). This was called the New People's Library, "a kind of left Home University Library", in V.G.'s words. Each book was 27,000 words or so in length and ran to about 96 pages.

> The aim has been to assume no previous knowledge whatever on the part of the reader : at the same time the books will, it is hoped, prove to be scientific—the simplification will be obtained by clarity of exposition.

The twenty-four volumes were issued monthly from July 1937 to July 1939. They became the most popular of the optional books and probably a higher proportion were read right through than was the case with the choices. Between 5,000 and 7,000 were taken by the Club each month. Here are some typical titles: Georges Sachs on *The Jewish Question*, Professor Farrington's *Civilisation of Greece and Rome*, John Mahon's book on *Trade Unionism*, and W. H. Thompson on *Civil Liberties*, were all very popular. Salvemini, who had written our first book on Italian fascism, *Under the Axe of Fascism*, now wrote a shorter book on *Italian Fascism*. Social questions were tackled by Brailsford in *Why Capitalism Means War*, and by Hannington in his *Short History of the Unemployed*. And so the list goes on. It formed a very creditable, informative, and interesting series. One of these books, *The Levellers and the English Revolution*, was by the distinguished scientist Dr Joseph Needham who is also a considerable authority in the history, religion and literature of the seventeenth century. He wrote under the pseudonym of Henry Holorenshaw.

There were also a good many short introductions to science among them and we should especially mention J. G. Crowther's *Science of Life*, H. C. Bibby on *The Evolution of Man and his Culture*, and John Rowland on *Understanding the Atom*.

It was in connection with the Educational books that V.G. launched a new form of *Associate* membership, in August 1937, aimed particularly at readers in industry and in the Trade Unions. It was apparent that the Club had not penetrated deeply enough into the organised working class and new methods were required to "extend and deepen our educational work among the industrial workers and particularly among the rapidly growing movement of militant youth." The aim was to meet the needs of those whose income could not extend to the monthly payment of 2s. 6d. per month (however strange this may seem in view of the generally higher standard of wages in 1970). There were also the many people who could not get through a book a month. It was, therefore, proposed to form study groups of people working together, or well known to one another, each of whom would receive each month the Educational book for the price of 6d. But the payment and distribution would be in the hands of a group leader or convenor who would collect 2d. a week from his members. This would allow him an additional 2d. a month per member for postal expenses in organising the group. The convenor would collect the books from the bookseller and pay him monthly. The group could then organise regular meetings and lectures to discuss the books; they would also be closely associated with the nearest regular Left Book Club Group and have the right to attend Summer Schools, conferences and other activities of the Club.

By October, twenty members had established circles of Associate members, ranging in size from six to forty people. V.G. had enlisted the help of William Paul, one of the earliest workers in the Communist Party, who had edited the *Sunday Worker* in 1925, but had long retired from full-time political work. It was hoped that Paul would develop the Club within the Trade Union movement, by means of his personal connections with leading officials. It would have been possible, for instance, to produce a special series of books on Trade Union and industrial matters. However, it was not found possible to develop this scheme and before long the Associate membership lapsed.

We also published a number of books designed to get beneath the level of day-to-day polemics to the more fundamental questions of political and social theory; and other books concerned with the historical development of Europe and Britain, which would show how the problem of the present had its root in the past. One of the most popular of these studies in history was A. L. Morton's *People's History of England*, which we made the choice for May 1938. Morton endeavoured to avoid the usual school textbook history which seems mainly concerned with kings, battles and treaties, and to write a history free from the bias, limitation and often blindness and sheer distortion of so much conventional writing. The result was a *social* as well as a political history of the English people. Morton also attempted to write a history exemplifying and applying that new and more scientific conception of the social and economic basis of society which alone makes sense and coherence out of the shape of things that have been. Among the Club's publications another important historical study was Hymie Fagan's *Nine Days that Shook England,* the story of the Peasants' Revolt of 1381.

Political theory was covered by several important books. Stephen Swingler wrote an *Outline of Political Thought Since the French Revolution.* Emile Burns and G. D. H. Cole both produced works on Marxist theory in *What is Marxism?* and *What Marx Really Meant,* thus giving us a study of Marxism from a Communist and non-Communist standpoint. An important analysis of the basic sickness of contemporary civilisation was R. H. Tawney's *Acquisitive Society*, the reprint of a "classic". Tawney, one of the most distinguished members of the staff of the London School of Economics, followed Ruskin and Carlyle in his severe criticism of an economic system which he described as "the negation of any system of thought or morals which can be described as Christian." While all the books were concerned either with some aspects of the international situation or with the problems of society, both theoretical and practical, a proportion dealt directly with the fascist danger and with Socialism. Here the breadth of view was considerable and extended from the Liberalism of Salvemini, Sir Ernest Simon and others, through the centre position of the Labour point of view, to the Marxist views of Strachey and Dutt.

Scientists were naturally drawn to the Club, but scattered as they were, in widely separated universities, their participation was mainly individual at first—often it was as speakers and lecturers that they really participated. However a group was eventually formed, and it got to work on an exhibition illustrating the "Frustration of Science". This took the form of pictures, graphs and diagrams showing the various ways in which science in our commercial civilisation is diverted from its true purpose of serving humanity.

The great success of the "Frustration of Science" exhibition led to its appearance at the Annual Meeting of the British Association. It was crowded, and the public meeting addressed by Professor Bernal was packed out. Every seat was occupied by members of the Association and also every inch of standing room. Bernal's theme was the progress of scientific discovery in relation to social development. A vigorous discussion followed among the assembled scientists.

In all the work of the group, Professors Levy, P. M. S. Blackett, and of course Bernal and Haldane played an active part and frequently spoke for the Club.

In September 1938 the choice was Haldane's book on A.R.P.—*Air Raid Precautions*. Haldane, speaking from first-hand experience of heavy bombing in Spain, advocated deep shelters as the safest precaution. Although deep shelters were only provided for certain governmental and administrative departments doing work of national importance, when bombing eventually started Londoners soon found that the safest place was the Underground. The stations were organised to receive the public in late evening, and people went home in the morning when the bombing was over. Haldane had a great deal to say about the perils and the possibilities of aerial bombardment. He had subjected himself to the most drastic experimental conditions of gassing, oxygen shortage and actual bombings, as this bit of verse by Sagittarius reminds us :

"What, Teacher, can that object be, inside a plate-glass drum?"
"It is Prof. Haldane whom you see, testing a vacuum"

"Why are they hurling bombs so near this shelter made of tin?"
"That is a bombproof test, I hear, Prof. Haldane is within"

"Oh, look! From yon balloon so high, what dangles large and limp?"
"It is Prof. Haldane we espy, air testing from a blimp"

"See drifting near the waterside that buoy of strange design!"
"That is Professor Haldane, tied, decoying of a mine.

On sea, on shore and in the air, protecting us from harm,
Prof. Haldane meets us everywhere—our scientific arm."

Science Groups soon began to spring up in Cambridge, Leeds, Birmingham, Leicester, Bristol, Derby and London. There was also a London Medical Group. Its first meeting took place in January 1939 with Professor Millais Culpin in the chair. There was a discussion on "Chinese Medicine". At subsequent meetings, the surgeon Mr Aleck Bourne, spoke on "Abortion", Dr Donald Hunter on "Industrial Health" and Professor Harold Levy on "The Biological Aspects of Anti-Semitism". Their meetings were well reported in the *Lancet* and the *British Medical Journal.*

Of all the activities of the Club beyond the original job of reading the books, the Summer Schools stand out for special consideration. They brought together members from all over the country, and from every kind of occupation and way of life. It was here that we felt the unity and purpose of the Club most strongly. All the schools were held in the lovely grounds of Digswell Park, but the third school ran an overflow specialising in drama, at Matlock.

The central feature of the second of these schools (1938), was

study based on a series of lectures by Strachey, Sir Norman
Angell, Maurice Dobb, Commander Edgar Young, Professor
Levy and myself. These took place every morning and were
followed by vigorous discussions. The afternoons were for swimming, games, walks, and lazy chats in the grounds. After tea
came individual lectures by Ellen Wilkinson, Dr Joseph Needham, Sir Richard Acland, Barbara Wootton, Professor Erich
Roll, Professor Farrington and many others. We covered an
immense range of subjects—Czechoslovakia, the Distressed
Areas, Philosophy, Economics and Politics, The United States,
Soviet Literature and Education. Extra lectures were given by
Sir Walter Layton, Sylvia Townsend Warner, R. Palme Dutt
and G. D. H. Cole.

As before, the feature of this Summer School which gave most
pure pleasure, was the after-dinner programme of music and
poetry. Here we were very fortunate. Everyone was ready to
help : the Blech Quartet came for one evening, Diana Poulton,
one of the few lutanists of that time, gave us a programme of
Elizabethan music; the London Musicians Group came down
for one evening, Unity Theatre performed for us, the Kino
Group presented films, more than one poet read his work to us—
Parry Jones, Jan van der Gucht, and Isabelita Alonso sang,
Sidney Harrison gave a lecture recital, and so it went on.

The third and last school came immediately before the outbreak of war. It was remarkable for the contributions of guests
from abroad. Dr Aurel Kolnai, with his unrivalled knowledge of
the philosophy of fascism, spoke on "The Fascist Threat to
Western Civilisation". There were visitors from France to speak
on the Popular Front, from North Africa, from the Colonies. It
was an international prelude of earnest consultation and conference before the iron doors closed.

From September 30th, 1938, the Munich surrender, to
September 3rd, 1939, when war was declared, was a time of
deep anxiety and growing peril. While all were aware of this
and were unceasing and desperate in their endeavours to avert
disaster, life went on much as usual. It was the same in regard to
the Club. There was intense activity in the way of meetings, rallies
and the distribution of leaflets, but all the while the discussion
groups went on; the writers of the Club books toured the provinces
and the Left Book Club Theatre Guild continued its work.

In January 1939, we were discussing Lord Addison's choice on *British Agriculture,* another subject concerned with our home problems. In July an analysis of the financial and industrial interests of the Conservative Members of Parliament, Simon Haxey's *Tory M.P.* Sir Ernest Simon contributed some solid material for intensive study on *The Smaller Democracies of Europe* (August 1939), which dealt with the steady social advance in Switzerland, Denmark, Norway and Finland from the point of view of a Liberal. This book was reviewed in the *Left News* by Eva Hubback, then Principal of Morley College.

The two annual rallies of the Club, to which members and not the general public came, had been an overwhelming success. The Club had grown larger and for the third rally we took the Empress Hall, Earls Court, on April 24th, 1939, probably the largest hall in Britain and seating 11,000. The platform was remarkable, for in addition to V.G. himself, Strachey, Harry Pollitt and the Dean of Canterbury, there was David Lloyd George, the veteran Liberal Statesman, now an old man. In his speech he called the Left Book Club "one of the most remarkable movements in the political field in two generations". Then there were Sir Stafford Cripps, Sir Norman Angell, Richard Acland and Wilfrid Roberts. One of the high points of the Rally was Paul Robeson who aroused a great outburst of enthusiasm when he sang.

The theme was the desperate need to persuade the French and British Governments ("the thirteenth Government I have seen," said Lloyd George, "and the worst.") of the urgent necessity of responding to the Russian invitation to join them in a last effort to restrain Hitler. "Three hundred million people of the earth," said Lloyd George, "have gone into slavery during the seven years' rule of our present political confederation. Why have we betrayed our trust so ignominiously?"

Nor did the meeting confine itself to a general analysis of the dangerous international situation. In ten minutes £600 was collected for the Club fund for crisis leaflets, and in addition the appeal by Richard Acland for volunteers and money for the return of Gabriel Carritt, Independent candidate in the Abbey division by-election, met with an immediate response.

This was the Club's last and biggest rally. We all knew we were at a turning point in history.

CHAPTER VIII

POLITICS AND EDUCATION—
THE LABOUR PARTY

ALL THROUGH 1938, and during the early part of 1939, the menace of war became more real; but life went on, and the Club grew and branched out in many ways.

Spain was very much in all our minds, and the Club published a twopenny pamphlet, *The Truth about Spain,* of which tens of thousands were sold by members. As the situation in Spain grew desperate, the Club organised a Food Ship and despatched it to Barcelona in February 1939.

On February 20th, 1938, Eden resigned over Chamberlain's further overtures to Mussolini. Eden had a very poor record over Spain. He had consistently supported the non-intervention agreement that allowed Hitler and Mussolini to support Franco, but denied even arms to the Spanish Government. The Club called a mass meeting in the Queen's Hall, with only five days' notice. It had a remarkable platform, perhaps the most representative in the whole history of the Club: the Dean of Canterbury, the Rev. A. D. Belden, the Moderator of the Presbyterian Church, Dr Maude Royden, Professor Levy, Professor Laski (Labour Party Executive), Richard Acland, M.P., Sir Charles Trevelyan, Richard Stokes, M.P., Professor Haldane and Sir Peter Chalmers Mitchell. The hall was packed, and I was deputed to lead the many hundreds, who could not get in, to Dr Belden's church in the Tottenham Court Road—Whitfield's Tabernacle. We marched through the streets and entirely filled the church. We at once started our meeting and, one by one, the principal speakers from the Queen's Hall came to address us.

It was during the autumn of that year that we carried through our biggest programme of rallies covering sixty-seven towns; in each one we took the Town Hall or the largest hall available. In addition Haldane, Bernal, Strachey and Major

Vernon carried through an A.R.P. Tour covering another forty towns. Koni Zilliacus, M.P., spoke at over fifty towns in the course of the tour, based on his book *Why we are Losing the Peace*.

On October 17th, 1938, a great meeting was held in the Queen's Hall as a "send off" to the Dean of Canterbury who, after his visit to Republican Spain, was going to America. The speakers once again extended across the whole political spectrum from D. N. Pritt, K.C., M.P., and Aneurin Bevan, M.P., to Dr Edith Summerskill, M.P., Ellen Wilkinson, M.P., the Rev. A. D. Belden and Professor Marrack.

By November 1938 the situation was desperate. The Club now printed and distributed the leaflet THERE IS GRAVE DANGER, written by V.G. and illustrated with a strategic map drawn by that genius of lucid cartography, J. F. Horrabin, a close friend of the Club and a regular speaker at its meetings. Eight million of this leaflet were distributed by the members.

Meanwhile there had loomed up on the horizon that "quarrel in a far-away country of which we know nothing", as Neville Chamberlain described it. It was the next victim marked down by Hitler, and it concerned us far more than the British Government realised. Czechoslovakia was in fact the Eastern bastion of Europe in the event of any thrust by Hitler towards Hungary, Yugoslavia, Romania or Russia, a highly industrialised country with a powerful armament industry. Chamberlain, it seemed, was prepared to open the door to the East for Hitler in the hope that his appetite would be satisfied by the expansion of Germany's *lebensraum* into Eastern Europe and the Ukraine. Thus France and Britain would be safe.

The growing interest in Czechoslovakia which these diplomatic and strategic moves aroused was immediately met by the Club in commissioning Lieut. Commander Edgar Young to write a book on this country. It was issued in June 1938, and was the subject of lectures all over the country by Dr Sindelkova, from Prague, and Commander Young himself. This was one of the most moving of the tours, because of the impending tragedy which we saw approaching this little democracy. Czechoslovakia was the last democracy in Eastern Europe, every other country had succumbed to dictatorship. In spite of the fact that there were internal strains between Czechs and

Slovaks, and that some sections of the Right were unwilling to face the desperate step of resistance to Hitler, it had a very genuine constitutional form of government and not merely a façade of parliamentary government as was the case with some countries. Its history goes back to the heroic national revival under John Huss, the religious leader of the fifteenth century. After 1918, when it emerged from the wreck of the Austrian Empire as a republic, it owed its independence to the philosopher statesman Tomas Masaryk and to Eduard Beneš. We knew its culture through the great educator Comenius and in recent times Smetana, the composer of *The Bartered Bride* and *Ma Vlast*. During the year of crisis leading up to Munich, the Club was a good deal better informed than the Government about Czechoslovakia.

But at this juncture it was the immediate threat to Spain with which we were concerned. The plight of the Republic had rapidly worsened, and now seemed all but hopeless. The attitude of the Labour leaders in this country was shown by their evasion of the overwhelming expression, at the Edinburgh Conference, of the Party's opposition to the non-intervention policy of the Government. But Transport House continued stubbornly along the path that led to Munich.

In 1938 the Club reached the highest point in its purely educational work. A good deal has already been said about the tours of our authors, the rapidly developing interest among artists, musicians, actors and scientists. Now we ventured on a new kind of study project—the Week-end School. The idea was to find a comfortable Guest House by the sea or in the country, in pleasant surroundings, and get twenty or thirty members to come down for the week-end, Friday night to Sunday evening. We would then get a lecturer to take over the programme and give a series of three or four talks, followed by discussion. There would be walks, bathing, tennis or some other form of relaxation; and often enough some music.

We published a list of Guest Houses where we would be welcome and at once the idea caught on. The pages announcing meetings, now running to six or seven in each issue of the *Left News* contained, as well, notices of these Week-end Schools. Among the speakers I notice the historian A. J. P. Taylor, Fred Peart (later Minister of Agriculture), Dr Edith Summerskill, M.P., the Earl of Listowel, Edward Upward, Dr Joseph

Needham, Frank Horrabin, Cecil Day Lewis, Pamela Hansford Johnson and Professor John Macmurray.

A typical centre for these Schools was Netherwood, Hastings, where that odd but charming literary figure Vernon Symonds kept a delightful table, for which his capable French wife was responsible, and ran every week-end a Club party with some distinguished guest speaker.

We began to get requests for regular classes in political theory, comparable to those provided by the W.E.A. We were by no means short of competent lecturers, and such classes were organised in Manchester, North London, Croydon, Southampton, Aberdeen, Stoke, Teddington and Central London.

The Syllabus covered three topics :

1. *An Introduction to Economics,* dealing with the development of modern capitalism and its characteristic features, the inevitability of crisis, capitalist remedies and their consequences, the growth of monopoly and economic imperialism.
2. *The Background of Politics.* The rise of the working-class movement, Chartism, Britain's industrial monopoly and its effect on politics and reformism, scientific socialism and the modern situation.
3. *Democracy and Current Problems.* The nature of the State. What is democracy? What is fascism? Capitalism's inevitable drive towards dictatorship and war. The People's Front.

These classes were restricted to twenty-four members. One of the lecturers was Stephen Swingler, who died in 1969, and was Barbara Castle's Assistant in the Ministry of Transport. He was at that time a W.E.A. Lecturer.

At the same time Speakers' classes were proceeding; their aim being to equip people to open discussion on the choice. For this purpose we prepared outline notes and syllabuses on every choice issued, and now with these better equipped leaders the quality of the group discussions greatly improved.

It is not possible to get very far in discussing social problems without raising the question of the *irrational*, and the psychology of persuasion and belief, or prejudice and mental blindness. The Club published several important books on these questions which members found stimulating. Reuben Osborn was one of

the first psychologists to deal with psychoanalysis in relation to
Marxist theory. This he had done in his *Freud and Marx* (the
Additional book for March 1937), and Francis Bartlett ap-
proached the subject from a different point of view in his
Sigmund Freud in November 1938.

A later choice, and one very relevant to the controversies of
the time, and the distortions of the press, was Amber Blanco
White's *The New Propaganda* (May 1939). Mrs White had
been for many years lecturer in Psychology at Morley College,
and, after the death of Mrs Eva Hubback, the Acting Principal.

In this useful book she reminded us of the "hidden persuaders",
the manipulation of public opinion by theories and philosophies
which really have an emotional or instinctive origin. It proved a
very popular choice.

Aurel Kolnai's *War Against the West* came out as an Additional in July 1939. V.G. had called it "the most important
book the Club has issued". It was an indictment of the Nazi
philosophy or rather of the many philosophies which prepared
the way for Hitler's religion of "blood and soil". In passage after
passage Kolnai quoted from the hundred or more makers of the
German mind for the past fifty years, culminating in the
immediate precursors of *Mein Kampf*. Advance copies had been
read by Lloyd George, Wickham Steed, formerly editor of *The
Times*, Professor Gilbert Murray and the Bishop of Durham. It
made a profound impression on all of them.

The book was a veritable encyclopaedia of Nazi philosophy,
and described a deliberate turning away from reason to the
cult of instinct, and especially the instinct of war and domination. This philosophy was being expounded for the twenty or
thirty years preceding Hitler's coming to power. It pervaded the
press, the schools, the universities and the literature of Germany.
It represented a fierce contempt for conscience, rules, moral
standards and human values.

Basically it was an attack on reason. Feeling and instinct
were to replace science as a sovereign and self-sufficing ground
for faith, hostile to all rational tests. It turns from external and
logical justification to "thinking with one's blood". Issued
originally as an Additional book in July 1938, *War Against the
West* was again issued as a Supplementary in September of the
same year.

In August the choice was *The Battle for Peace* by Elwyn Jones (to become Solicitor General), and, in the Educational Series, Brailsford's *Why Capitalism Means War*.

In the first year of the Left Book Club the Labour Party had regarded it with cool but not hostile interest. Mr Attlee sent a friendly message to the Albert Hall Rally. But his tolerant attitude did not last very long. The Labour Party strongly disapproved of the Club's policy of providing a common platform for all shades of opinion in its campaign for Collective Security; it also disapproved of our publication of books by Strachey, Dutt and Hannington, who were communists or near communists; and they wished, if that were possible, to prevent members of the Labour Party reading books expressing views contrary to those of Transport House. As we shall see, they went so far, eventually, as to threaten members of the Club with expulsion from the Labour Party.

The Club, for its part, never, on any occasion attacked the Labour Party, though it frequently controverted the arguments of certain of its leaders and criticised its policy, as many well known Labour members of parliament also did. Criticism is not forbidden in the Labour Party, as debates at the Annual Conference and vigorous disagreements with various Party decisions by loyal members clearly demonstrate. The Club endeavoured in every way to strengthen the Party and to augment its membership. Very many Club members were persuaded to join.

In June 1938, John Strachey wrote an article in the *Left News* on "The Peace Alliance", based on Mr Attlee's own well known statement on the Popular Front in the book he wrote for the Club, *The Labour Party in Perspective*. Attlee had written : "I would not myself rule out such a thing [i.e. a Popular Front] as an impossibility in the event of the imminence of a world crisis." Strachey argued that there was no other way of checking the Government's dangerous policy of appeasement apart from a combination of all forces, Liberal, Labour, Communist, and people of no party at all, on this single issue. Only if war could be averted could we get down to the constructive policies of social reform in which we might well wish to take different roads; therefore, "let us first secure the firm peace, which we all want and without which none of us can do anything." But the

Labour Party even went so far as to say that to join forces with Liberals for this purpose was to "give up socialism".

Strachey concluded his article with these words :

These then are the arguments, as I see them, in favour of common action between all those who will oppose the Chamberlain and Halifax policy of the Fascist Alliance. The Peace Alliance is a proposed method by which the Labour Party can put itself at the head of the Progressive forces of Britain, and by doing so occupy a dominant position in the public life of Great Britain. By seizing this opportunity the Chamberlain Government could be defeated in time to save the world from Fascism and War. If the leaders of the Labour Party can suggest an alternative method, then let them tell us of it. Until and unless they do so we can do no other than to press on with the task of winning Liberals, Labour men, Communists, and men and women of no party allegiance, to the cause of standing together for their mutual preservation from Fascism and war.

The Club repeatedly made overtures to the Labour Party. In August 1937, Harold Laski, on behalf of the Club, offered the Party two entire pages in the *Left News* each month, and offered to throw the whole strength of the Club behind the Labour Party's autumn campaign. It went further, and offered to devote two entire issues to the Labour Party, two written articles on all the major political issues by their own people. This would have reached an active membership of 40,000, and cost the Club £1,000.

The offer was flatly rejected. There could be no co-operation, said Dalton, unless the Labour Party secured control of the Club. Despite this rebuff, the Club continued its support for Labour because, as Strachey said, "Let us make no mistake about it, whatever we may wish for, or hope for, the fact remains that the whole future of democracy, peace and decency in Britain depends upon the preservation, development and revival of the Labour movement." For the Labour Party to argue that the leadership and its policies must never be criticised seemed to us no way of helping the movement.

We continued to try to find Labour people, either members or sympathisers, to write books for us from their own position, as the Liberals were doing. They appeared to have nothing to say. Very little indeed came at that time, from any publisher, from the Labour Right, which seemed to be intellectually exhausted.

As the Club developed the groups were able to render the local Labour Parties considerable service. We advised new members, who were not members of any party, to join the party nearest to their views, which was in most cases the Labour Party. Hundreds did so. Dormant "constituency parties", with declining numbers and no activities, were galvanised into action by an influx of fresh members, anxious to get to work. In fact the largest single group of club members belonged to the Labour Party, and many of its most eminent authors, such as Laski, Cole, Cripps, Noel-Baker, Ellen Wilkinson and Attlee came from its ranks. But Bevin declared that the main object of the Club was "to undermine and destroy the Trade Unions and the Labour Party as an effective force", and Herbert Morrison complained that it was interfering with the Labour Party's "consistent ordered work". He went further and threatened disciplinary action against those working side by side with members of other parties for peace and collective security. These Popular Front activities were an anathema.

This was not the end. The Labour Party started a rival organisation, the "Labour Book Service", which had a very short life; and it accompanied this by a threat to all members of the Labour Party to the effect that unless they refrained from buying the books of the Left Book Club, they might find themselves liable to expulsion. The threat was contained in an official letter sent out, by Mr G. R. Shepherd, the National Agent of the Labour Party, to all secretaries of borough, divisional and local Labour parties.

This meant, in effect, that the Labour Party proposed to control the reading of its million or so readers, and it aroused a storm of protest including a dignified letter from Sir Charles Trevelyan, the former President of the Board of Education, who said that "it was an inexpressible tragedy that, at this moment when the influence of the executive ought to be used for drawing together by inspiration and reconciliation all possible sections of anti-Chamberlain opinion, it should be spending its time in disintegrating the Labour Party by threats, expulsions, and anathemas".[1]

Mr Shepherd had spoken of "activities embarrassing to Con-

[1] *Left News* (April 1939).

stituency Labour Parties". What were these activities? He went on to explain : "One group has taken the initiative in holding public meetings on Spain, Czechoslovakia, etc., and in directing attention to the problems of the distressed areas. *For some years there has been no activity of this kind in the district*" (our italics). Gollancz replied that to this charge the Club must plead guilty. "It is true that Left Book Club members of some Labour Parties have in district after district shown the greatest enthusiasm in recreating socialist and progressive activity of every kind. If this is an embarrassment to local Labour Parties why then we must say roundly it is high time such parties should be embarrassed. It will not be until they cease, and Transport House ceases, to 'be embarrassed' by such activities that there is the slightest hope for the Labour movement of this country."[2]

It was before this onslaught that the Club had intervened to very good purpose in helping to secure the victory of the Liberal journalist and popular broadcaster Vernon Bartlett as an Independent Progressive in the by-election at Bridgwater in 1938. In a situation in which nothing was being done and there was much apathy and reluctance to take action, it was the Left Book Club Groups of Minehead, Bath, Taunton, Street and Glastonbury, Clevedon, and even North Somerset that were instrumental in getting the campaign going and carrying it to a successful conclusion. It was a striking Popular Front victory of the combined Labour and Liberal forces. The Club Groups had sprung to life in areas here where the Labour organisation was quite dead. There is no doubt whatever that they were responsible for getting Labour on its feet in this locality, bringing into existence the Minehead and District Labour Party and the Watchet Labour Party. The personality of Richard Acland, a West Country man himself, a Liberal and dedicated to the Popular Front, played a decisive role in this affair, whose success was entirely due to the bridge that was built between Liberalism and Labour by the Left Book Club.

In May 1938, the Club had launched a new enterprise : the publication of a series of paper-covered booklets at the very low price of twopence. The first was what we called the "Twopenny

[2] *Left News* (**April 1939**).

Strachey". The idea was to put on sale at this absurdly low price what was in fact a small book very clearly and popularly written on some topic that would catch the imagination of thousands, indeed of tens of thousands. In the year 1900 there had been a brilliant example of this—Blatchford's *Britain for the British,* a well-written and lively presentation of the case for socialism, running to 150 pages and selling for threepence. It had an enormous circulation, and made more socialists than any other book published in the English language. The "Twopenny Strachey" attempted to do the same thing. Gollancz had received the manuscript of a book on socialism written by Strachey for the Educational Series. It seemed to him "a little masterpiece—crystal clear, requiring not the slightest knowledge of politics, economics and history for the understanding of it." It was written in an engaging style and "so persuasive as to be unanswerable." It consisted of 30,000 words, or about half the length of the ordinary novel, making a book of one hundred pages.

V.G. calculated that if he could sell 100,000 copies it could be put on the market for twopence. How to do this? Could we turn the whole membership of the Club into a *distributing machine* by which a book like this could be passed on to the general public? If this were possible it might provide the first approach to the indifferent, the ignorant and even to the hostile. It was an idea worth trying out. (V.G. even thought that at so cheap a price members might give it away—in the event this was never necessary.)

The proposal was made in February 1938, and members were asked how many they would take. By April the orders coming in gave promise of an edition of 100,00 at twopence. It was published on May 9th. In the first year of its issue 250,000 copies had been sold. One convener ordered 2,000 and his group easily sold them. Mobile units canvassed their districts and sold them from door to door. Open-air meetings were held and the booklet sold to those attending.

V.G. always laid the emphasis on the need for more knowledge, and the Left Book Club, whatever its other activities, never slackened in the circulation of books which helped to clarify the complicated issue of the day and to provide "the facts without which no useful conclusions would be arrived at". The membership, V.G. reminded them in the April issue of the

THE HITLER MENACE

Don't be fooled

by the pretence that the crisis is anything to do with the "sufferings" of the Germans in Czechoslovakia (who are well treated).

If you have been fooled

consider this: on May 7th, 1938, the *Economist* (sober business journal) said: "The Germans in Italy (S. Tyrol) have been perhaps the worst treated subject minority in post-war Europe." On the same day Hitler said the frontier between Germany and Italy should be forever unchangeable—*i.e.*, he had no intention of demanding self-determination" for the Germans ill-treated by his ally Italy!

Why does Hitler want Czechoslovakia destroyed?

Because his real aim is to annihilate France, with a view to world domination.

Would Britain then be safe?

NO

The point is this: if Czechoslovakia remains strong, Russia, in alliance with her, can prevent Germany concentrating all her forces on France: but if Czechoslovakia goes, there is a barrier between Germany and Russia, who would then find it far more difficult to help France.

[TURN OVER

Does the present "... Plan" smash Czechoslovakia?

Yes: it deprives her of her mountain frontiers, her magnificent fortifications and an immense part of her industry. She would be powerless, whether "guaranteed" or not (we know now the worth of "guaranties").

Why do we accuse Hitler thus?

Because he has openly stated this aim again and again.; In *Mein Kampf*, the Bible of Nazi Germany, which sells at the rate of a million copies a year (every German couple has to get it on marrying; it is a textbook in every school) he writes: "Germany . . . sees a remedy only in the annihilation of France . . . so that afterwards our people can finally have the possibility of expansion in other places."

Will giving way to Hitler give us peace?

NO: if it makes World war certain. In view of his declared aims, Hitler will go on with aggression after aggression, until he challenges France (which means also ourselves) with immensely greater resources than at present, and with his rear safe. We should probably be defeated.

Will it give us even immediate peace?

Most improbable. The Nazi press (completely controlled by Hitler) is already crying out for the elimination of the entire Czechoslovakian State (Hitler always raises his demands). To-day's *Star* (September 20th) says "Whose turn next?" Hungary and Rumania getting anxious." Every minority in Central and S.E. Europe will be on the move. General ferment: mobilisations; sooner or later, general war.

If we stand firm

we, the French, and the Russians, even at this eleventh hour, and say we will not let Hitler destroy Czechoslovakia by armed might, will he fight? Most improbable, for the superiority of the three of us *now* is enormous. And if he were mad enough to challenge us, he would certainly be defeated.

Printed at the Farleigh Press (T.U. all depts.), 27-29 Cayton Street, E.C.1.

[TURN OVER

Left News (1938), "are welded into a whole by a particular interest, a particular belief—by a pursuit of that *knowledge* that will give them direction in the common fight against war and fascism".

This highly successful venture was followed by two more twopennies: *The Truth about Spain,* and *How to be Safe from Air Raids* based on Haldane's *A.R.P.* In March 1939, appeared the "Twopenny Dean"—the Dean of Canterbury's *Act Now: An Appeal to the Mind and Heart of Britain.* It was a passionate plea for socialism as an expression of the Christian ethic. It sold 200,000.

The last of the series was the "Penny Gollancz", entitled *Is Mr Chamberlain Saving Peace?* V.G. answered that he was not!

One of the Club leaflets has already been mentioned; it had an almost incredible circulation. Three were put out in all. Of the two chief leaflets, ten million were distributed. This indicated the enthusiastic effort of the members, who threw themselves into the campaign with notable energy and devotion.

The Hitler Menace (September 1938) declared that surrender to Hitler over Czechoslovakia would make war certain:

> If we stand firm, we, the French and the Russians, even at this eleventh hour, and say we will not let Hitler destroy Czechoslovakia by armed might, will he fight? Most improbable, for the superiority of the three of us *now* is enormous. And if he were mad enough to challenge us, he would certainly be defeated.

Two million were distributed. The Spain leaflet *There is Grave Danger* was issued in November of the same year, when the Government was considering granting belligerent rights to Franco. It was issued in conjunction with the *Tribune* and the Spanish Emergency Committee. No charge was made for the leaflets, the money being raised independently. Nearly eight million were distributed by the Club alone.

V.G. envisaged a continuous process of leaflet propaganda over the years; but it is doubtful whether this would have been possible, or indeed desirable, had the Club pursued its main

Facsimile
reproduction of
the 'Spain' leaflet

THERE IS
GRAVE DANGER

that the Government will, during the next week or so

**ACTUALLY HELP THE FASCISTS TO STARVE
THE SPANISH PEOPLE INTO SURRENDER**

This would happen if they agreed to the Granting of Belligerent Rights to Franco, which he desires in order to enable him to blockade Spanish Government ports.

DO YOU THINK IT JUST—after the Spanish Government has held out year after year with incredible heroism, and is now sending away all its foreign volunteers, in spite of the attacks from all the troops and aeroplanes Germany and Italy have still got in Spain—that

We, Great Britain, should now help to defeat them by starving their children?

Our Foreign Secretary, Lord Halifax, has said in the House of Lords that "Mussolini has always made it plain from the time of the first conversations with the British Government, that for reasons known to all of us, whether we approve them or not, he was not prepared to see General Franco defeated."

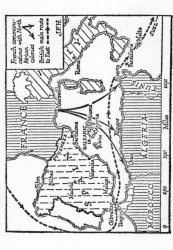

P.T.O.

Why should WE help Mussolini to win another victory at our expense?

Whatever you may think about Spain,

REMEMBER OUR OWN PERIL

Our existence depends on food. Our food comes mainly from overseas. Any hostile power in control of Spain would, in the event of war, endanger the greater part of our food supplies and so

STARVE US INTO SURRENDER!

Mr. Chamberlain, in spite of the "appeasement" at Munich, tells us that it is vital that we should

RE-ARM AGAINST POSSIBLE DANGERS

What dangers? There can only be an attack upon us by the Fascist Powers.

ISN'T IT LUNACY

In the very act of re-arming with one hand, with the other to present the Fascists with the possibility of Starving Us?

AND REMEMBER THIS

Britain is the home of liberty and democracy. The greater the numbers of democracies that are conquered by Fascism, the greater becomes our own peril. Czechoslovakia has gone. Why now

**DELIBERATELY HELP THE FASCISTS TO
CONQUER SPAIN?**

No belligerent rights for Franco!

All foreigners must be withdrawn from Spain!

Let the Spaniards make peace with one another!

Act immediately if you value the future of our country!

Fill up and post to your M.P. If you do not know his name, post it to "The M.P. for ..../............... (put the name of your district), House of Commons, London." Better still, write to him personally on the subject.

I agree with the views set out in this leaflet, and, as one of your constituents, urge you to support these demands.

Name...

Address...Date..............

educational task. These leaflets were drawn up by V.G. with immense care; he used to sit up half the night, writing draft after draft to get the right emphasis, to convey the most telling facts convincingly, to strike the urgent note effectively.

The third and last leaflet was issued in April 1939 after a leaflet fund had been started at the huge Empress Hall Rally. £600 was collected that night, and more contributions poured in. This was the *Save Peace* leaflet, calling for a collective security agreement between Britain, France and Russia. One and three quarter million leaflets were distributed in a few days.

The Government was slowly and reluctantly moving towards the Moscow consultations which ultimately broke down. When the decision to send a Government delegate to Moscow was reached the leaflet was revised to support active negotiation, and many more were distributed.[3] Every endeavour to persuade the Government to negotiate an agreement failed. The British and French delegates refused to accept the Russian offer of military support. The Russians immediately signed their own Non-Aggression pact with Hitler.

[3] *Left News* (May 1939).

CHAPTER IX

FALLEN BASTIONS

THE LEFT BOOK CLUB'S main purpose had always been work for the alliance for peace and to contribute all that it could in the way of education, information and persuasion to that end. This was a desperately urgent matter when the Club came into existence in 1936. V.G. wrote, in October 1938 :

> It was clear to me that we were being swept at an irresistible pace towards destruction, and it seemed pitiful and absurd that peace lovers, whether they called themselves Liberals or Communists or Labour Party men, should refuse to consider some sort of unity in the face of this menace.[1]

The surrender to Hitler at Munich seemed to us all, as it did to most realistic politicians, to give *carte blanche* to Hitler to do whatever he wanted in Eastern Europe, and everyone knew that his open and frequently proclaimed demand had been for the domination of the Balkans and Eastern Europe and the conquest of the Ukraine. Indeed it was suspected that the Government hoped that the explosion would take place *eastwards* and leave the West at peace and unscathed.

It must not be supposed that the Club stood alone in its rejection of this policy. On the contrary, while the peace-loving public, ignorant of the underlying facts and gravely misled by the Press, was only too glad to leave things alone and let the "far away countries" about which they knew nothing, suffer their fate, a stalwart minority of distinguished men and women of affairs were also campaigning against appeasement. Some of them were Conservatives or Liberals, others Independent. They were taking the same view as the Club on the issue of appeasement; and after Munich and its disastrous consequences, more

[1] *Left News.*

and more of those who had applauded Chamberlain also saw the question in this light. Those who had from the first opposed the Government were vindicated.

There were many others outside the world of politics, scientists like Chalmers Mitchell of the Zoological Society, philosophers like Professor Collingwood of Oxford, musicians like Vaughan Williams, whose sympathy was entirely with whomsoever was working for collective security at that time and opposing concessions to Hitler.

But the opposition from these quarters, even from political figures such as Sir Walter Layton, Sir Archibald Sinclair, Wickham Steed (the former editor of *The Times*) and Lady Violet Bonham Carter, not to mention Churchill and his friends, failed to influence the Government in the slightest degree. In Lady Violet's words, "Leaden despair descended upon us as we realised our helplessness." Many were surprised and indignant at the refusal of the Press to report their speeches. The Club also found its meetings ignored, no matter how large or impressive the audience or how distinguished the platform. We might pack the Albert Hall, and the Queen's Hall for the overflow; we might fill the Empress Hall with 11,000 people and also turn many away; we might have Lloyd George as the principal speaker—the meeting would be ignored by the press, and so would equally successful meetings in the largest halls all over the country.

Of course it was not official censorship. It was more like an open conspiracy of silence to blot out whatever conflicted with the political aims of the Government. Leading articles were appearing in the national press arguing that Czechoslovakia must be abandoned because it would be better to sacrifice a minority rather than imperil the peace of Europe. V.G. commented bitterly that they must have known that the real issue was Hitler's plans for world domination which he had publicly proclaimed again and again :

If they knew them, and deliberately deceived the public, they are utterly base : if they did not know them their contemptible ignorance is matched only by the almost inconceivable levity which allows men so ignorant to write about politics at all.[2]

[2] *Left News* (November 1968).

Whatever their intentions, the efforts of the pacifists power-fully reinforced the policy of appeasement. The Peace Pledge Union and Middleton Murry, Dr Joad and his immensely popular paperback *Why War?*, Bertrand Russell's *Which Way to Peace?*, Aldous Huxley, Vera Brittain, and many others, all helped to build a strong feeling against an ultimate threat of war to check Hitler.

There was a pacifist tendency within the Club, but not a strong one. We published one book which attempted to deal with the question. It was *The Citizen Faces War* by the Don-ingtons, which stated the case both for and against pacifism fairly and sympathetically. It started from the pacifist point of view but it came down eventually on the side of collective security. This was the position of Victor Gollancz himself who had never concealed his loathing for war or his instinctive sympathy for pacifism, but now felt compelled to give his support and that of the Club to collective security, security based in the last resort on force. V.G. in the *Left News* for March (1937) asked members to re-read Strachey's "topic of the Month" for January, which was a discussion of "what our attitude should be if war comes in spite of our effort to avert it". Strachey believed that the pacifist position was mistaken. Gollancz agreed: "I profoundly believe that in the present phase of world history pacifism is not merely mistaken, but one of the most dangerous forces which anti-fascism has to face."[3] But in the minds of some members there was a strong desire to inter-pret the policy of collective security as one which, since it aimed at the *prevention* of war, could not itself contemplate war in the last resort. This was seldom stated in so many words, but the policy advocated was to explain what fascism was, to work for a unified front, to get as many nations as possible to oppose Hitler, *then Hitler would not dare to challenge us*.

As the possibility of actual war drew near, in the Munich days, V.G. himself, abandoning his earlier emphatic rejection of pacifism, flinched from the last step. His pacifism, previously asleep, was beginning to stir. Could military resistance—killing your enemy—ever be right? That on the one hand; but on the other the *half*-conscious assumption "that if prevention didn't come off, then we must fight."

He was not alone in this deep reluctance to face the ultimate

[3] *Left News* (March 1937).

question. He says, "I held in suspense, so to speak, the sufficiently obvious fact that these methods implied—given their failure to prevent war, implied in a logic that was also honour, just the violent resistance that I was on the point of repudiating. . . . This is the sort of muddle I was in."[4]

The reply of course was that those who did not repudiate the ultimate resort to a military threat were prepared to face the price of war rather than yield to Nazi aggression because *only by doing so did they expect to keep the peace!*

It was just after publishing the Donington's book that we considered producing a more careful and thorough examination of the pacifist case. I was asked to write something; and early in 1938 submitted my *Case Against Pacifism* to V.G. It was accepted and proofed (in paper-bound page form). Then came Munich and V.G.'s own "Thoughts after Munich", his Editorial in the *Left News* for November 1938. V.G.'s latent pacifism, when confronted with an exhaustive rebuttal, caused him to feel the deepest reluctance to have my book published. That reluctance was expressed in the *Left News* when he excused himself from a discussion of the fundamental issue of pacifism on the ground that space did not permit. Later he confessed that when he said this he was "shirking : never more obviously"[5] the real issue.

So the publication of the *Case Against Pacifism* was delayed, and postponed, until war overtook us and it was too late. Then it was, unhappily, withdrawn, to my deep disappointment.[6] But I knew that for V.G. at that time to publish a rebuttal of pacifism would be to deny his own deepest instinct of antagonism to war.

In February 1939 the Club published *Fallen Bastions* by G. E. R. Gedye, who had been *The Times* correspondent in Central Europe for many years. He was on the spot first in Vienna, and then in Prague right through the crisis. In his book he pointed out that, strategically, to throw open the whole of the Eastern flank of Europe, abandoning an immensely powerful

---

[4] *More for Timothy,* p. 355.
[5] *More for Timothy,* p. 376.
[6] With V.G.'s consent it was submitted to Allen & Unwin who published it in 1940. A special paper-back was made available to club members and members of the Workers Educational Association.

line of defence and disbanding a large, efficient and powerful Czech army, was, from a military point of view, suicide.

This was also the conclusion of many commentators on the extreme right. R. W. Seton Watson declared that "Czechoslovakia is the strategic key to hegemony in Europe, quite apart from any sympathies or antipathies which you may have for the only state in Eastern Europe which has been able to maintain a system of free democratic and representative government."[7]

Konni Zilliacus, the M.P. for Gateshead, in his Club book, *The Road to War,* and R. P. Dutt in *World Politics,* were arguing that Hitler was aware that Britain would never go to war to stop him recovering the German speaking territories lost at Versailles, and uniting Austria with the Third Reich; and that Hitler calculated that as with each such step his strength would grow, by the time he came to the last, which Britain and France would suddenly see as fatal to them, they could be, relative to his military superiority, too weak to resist.[8]

These warnings proved only too accurate. After annexing the Sudetenland, Hitler proceeded to march into Prague and occupy the whole country. Chamberlain had guaranteed Czech integrity at Munich, but he appeared to have no intention of implementing his engagement. The reason that he gave was that "no guarantee could be valid of a state that did not exist."

When Czechoslovakia fell the Germans obtained 1,500 Czech planes, 469 tanks, and the Skoda armament works, and put out of commission 56 divisions. Chamberlain had argued that by 1939 we might be ready to meet Hitler's strength, yet in the event Hitler armed at full speed and we at a snail's pace; and nothing that we could do could compensate for the loss of the

[7] *Czechoslovak Broadsheet,* R. W. L. Seton Watson (No. 1, July 1939).

[8] It appeared when, after the War, we gained possession of the *Documents on German Foreign Policy,* and also had access to the *Documents on British Foreign Policy,* that these conclusions were correct. But matters were even worse. Halifax, Nevile Henderson, our ambassador in Berlin, and Chamberlain had repeatedly assured Hitler that we did not propose to interfere in his occupation of Czechoslovakia, or his plans for expansion into Eastern Europe and Russia. It was clear that their policy was to win an alliance with Germany, a Four Power Union (Germany, Italy, France and Britain), at the expense of Eastern Europe and Russia. It was from the first never a question of armaments, or any intention of resisting Hitler, it was a matter of long term policy which accepted and encouraged Hitler's Eastern European expansion.

Czech army and her armament industry. Those who opposed appeasement believed that the Western powers could have stopped Hitler but were not prepared to. And then, when at last they had to face him, they had the will but not the power.

From now until the outbreak of war the members of the Club were sick with disquiet. All that the Club had struggled for seemed lost, and the future was indeed dark.

CHAPTER X

THE CLUB AND COMMUNISM

IN HIS "Thoughts after Munich", Gollancz expressed his growing conviction that "the communists were far more influential in the Club than they ought to have been, if indeed this could have been avoided."[1] He had, in fact, increasingly felt that the Club's support for Soviet Communism and communist policies generally was involving it in a disregard for objective truth, in acceptance of the doctrine that the end justifies the means, and in the toleration of coercion and violence as inevitable in the transition to socialism.

It will be worth while to ask whether this was indeed the case, and if so to what extent and in what way the Club was influenced by communism.

There were in fact very few communists among the authors of the Monthly Choice. Strachey, the most influential, was not a member of the Party, and his views rapidly began to diverge from Marxism in the direction of monetary reform. Dutt's *World Politics* had been published before the Club was started and only later was issued as an Additional book. Hannington wrote only factual studies of poverty and unemployment. There was also Pat Sloan's *Soviet Democracy*, and Emile Burns edited the *Handbook of Marxism,* a volume of selections from the Marxist classics which proved as useful to critics of Marxism as to those more sympathetic to it. Both were influential but there was nothing in these books advocating violence or dictatorship, or counselling deceit or the doctrine that "the end justifies the means".

As to the influence of communist speakers on the Club platforms, there were in the first place very few of them on the platform of the big rallies. One recalls Pollitt, Strachey and Hannington. But they were almost always speaking on the social problem in England or on such issues as Spain, China or

[1] *More for Timothy*, p. 357.

Czechoslovakia, or on the menace of fascism and the danger of appeasement. I can recall no occasion on which their Labour or Liberal associates on the platform took exception to what they said. They spoke to the Club's agenda, not on those issues which would have involved the full communist position, which lay beyond the immediate scope of the Club's activity.

As for the groups, as we have shown, large numbers of members were newcomers to politics. Some eventually joined the Communist Party, but more joined the Labour Party. The occasional sectarian who entered a group to flog the Party line, acted contrary to that line, was extremely unpopular, and soon disappeared.

The Communist Party branches had little direct association with the Club. For the most part their members had too many branch responsibilities, and were too busy with their own campaigns to take on the endless tasks which membership of a Left Book Club group would entail. Some did, no doubt, but in most cases the energetic spirits were newcomers.

The Club's interest in communism had three sources : in the first place there was a growing belief that in Russia we could see the socialist alternative to capitalism with its unemployment, economic crisis and poverty, coming into being and establishing itself. Secondly, fascism itself was seen not simply as an outburst of nationalism and militarism but as the capitalist alternative to socialism. Laski had been arguing for some years[2] that the rise of the new dictatorships was due to the capitalist fear of democracy taking the socialist road, and also to the belief that the only solution to their economic difficulties was to be found in economic expansion—a war for *lebensraum*. In Hitler's case this was to be found in Eastern Europe—in Russia.[3] Thirdly, the only way to prevent the spread of fascist power throughout Europe was an alliance of all the democratic and peace-loving powers, along with Russia. The Popular Front, which was being advocated in France and Britain, was to be an alliance of all

[2] Laski, *Democracy in Crisis* (Allen & Unwin, 1933).
[3] Hitler wrote: "For Germany the only possibility for carrying out a sound territorial policy lay in the winning of new land in Europe itself. This could only happen at the cost of Russia. We stop the march to the South and West of Europe and turn our eyes towards the land in the East. We can only think in the first instance of Russia and her border states." (*Mein Kampf,* quoted in Friends of Europe Publications, No. 34.)

democrats to present a solid front against fascism both on the home front and internationally.

The Popular Front was defending democracy against the onward march of fascism, in order that it might be free to pursue the constitutional road to socialism or to any alternative policy that a free people might prefer. But Socialists believed that the policy of a Popular Front would certainly mean a struggle with our own reactionary elements, who were giving support to fascism because it seemed to them to be the only alternative to socialism.

Beyond these considerations was the over-riding importance of the inclusion of Soviet Russia in an alliance of collective security against the growing threat of war. In the long run, it was this united front that we had to depend on to win the war when or if it came.

It was for these reasons that the Club looked hopefully towards Russia, and that it was prepared to do its best to hold back the Nazi imperialist drive into Eastern Europe. To prevent the victory of fascism was both to preserve our own political freedom and to defend the new social order which Hitler threatened with destruction. Both those who believed that democracy would choose socialism and those who thought it would pursue a non-socialist policy of reform, could agree to defend the liberty of democratic freedom.

There was one serious difficulty about this attitude to Russia. The communists appeared to some to have abandoned democratic institutions, and to be maintaining socialism by force, allowing no legal opposition, no political discussion, and no freedom to dissent. Moreover was it not likely that the Communist Parties of the West would attempt to establish socialism here after the same pattern?

The communist defenders of the Soviet Union replied that the real freedoms established by socialism : freedom from unemployment, want, and exploitation; the opening up of a vast range of opportunity for all; the State's care for children, for education, for health; the disappearance of the false money values and parasitism of the society run by and in the interests of the rich, fully compensated for the forcible suppression of capitalist institutions and political parties, and indeed could not be secured without such measures. They went on to argue that political liberty and freedom of speech under capitalism were shams, for the ruling class controlled effectively all the means of information and had other means of intimidating and hoodwinking the masses.

In many of the books on Russia, issued by the Club, and also in a series of articles in the *Left News,* these ideas were vigorously and persuasively set forth. Ivor Montagu wrote in the *Left News* the articles entitled *The U.S.S.R. Month by Month,* on "The Land of the Free", "Riches", "The Trials", "Red Empire", and "The Red Army". While Strachey wrote on "Democracy and Freedom", and "The Guilty" (again referring to the Trials); Pat Sloan wrote the Club choice on *Soviet Democracy,* and the *Left News* published a full summary of the Stalin Constitution, and a long review of the Webbs' *Soviet Communism, a new Civilisation,* which described the new economic and social system, though it ignored the question of who administered it and how much genuine constitutional liberty there was to participate, to criticise, to make the effective decisions.

The main interest of the Club in Russia was not in the machinery of government and democratic procedure, but in the social and economic progress, for which surprising evidence was coming in.

Thus the Five Year Plan had been brought to a much more successful end than most people expected. Russia was equipping herself with a heavy industry and machine building plants without loans or capitalist investment from abroad. The standard of living was slowly rising. On the other hand, in Europe and America we had suffered a disastrous economic collapse and had by no means completely recovered. There was still poverty and unemployment.

As the tide of extreme anti-Soviet prejudice receded it began to appear to many sympathisers as though the socialist dream were really coming true. In contrast to the capitalist philosophy of acquisition and competition, with the inevitable social strife, economic crisis, and wars for markets, people began to see in Russia the harbinger of the new world of their long frustrated hopes.

A number of books published by the Club persuasively described the Soviet scene—a picture of this new world, long concealed by hostile propaganda or the sheer suppression of the truth. These books were :

Changing Man: The education system in the U.S.S.R.
                              by Beatrice King
Socialised Medicine in the Soviet Union
                              by Dr Sigerist
The Position of Women in the U.S.S.R.
                              by G. N. Serebrennikov
Soviet Communism, a New Civilisation
                              by Sidney and Beatrice Webb
Comrades and Citizens
                              by Seema Rynin Allan
The Socialist Sixth of the World
                              by The Dean of Canterbury

The tide ran strongly in favour of the new socialist order.

V.G. himself was profoundly impressed by the first lectures of the Dean of Canterbury, and one recalls his return to the office after his own visit to Russia in 1937 and how he gathered the entire staff together to hear his enthusiastic and infectious account of what he at that time *did* see as a "new civilisation". When he first brought the Dean into the Club and arranged many meetings for him, he described in the *Left News* the immense force and conviction that the Dean gave to his picture of the "Socialist Sixth of the Earth". V.G. spoke of him then in terms of real appreciation. It was much later that he became more critical. There was some justification perhaps for this more critical attitude, but the Dean did bring a warm appreciation and a new understanding of a Russia which hardly anyone knew much about, and which was sadly misrepresented and misjudged by many people.

Between 1936 and 1939 the Left Book Club issued fifteen books dealing with the Soviet Union. Among them we have already mentioned the Webbs' *Soviet Communism*, a huge book of 1,200 pages which we distributed at five shillings as an Additional book. It was reviewed in the *Left News* by Bernard Shaw. Over-praised by those inclined to see only the best, it was later more severely criticised than its distinguished Fabian authors deserved.

Dr Sigerist, Professor of the History of Medicine at Johns Hopkins, U.S.A., wrote *Socialised Medicine in the Soviet Union* for us. Its balanced conclusions coincided with those of many other medical experts including Dr Edith Summerskill, M.P., and Sir Arthur Newsholme (Principal Medical Officer of the Local Government Board), who could not be regarded as in any way biased in a pro-Soviet direction.

Beatrice King's *Changing Man: The Education System in the U.S.S.R.*, was a careful and accurate account of the Russian Schools. Subsequent visits by such authorities as the delegation led by Professor Jeffreys of the Institute of Education, London, resulted in equally favourable estimates of educational progress in the Soviet Union.[4]

Later came the first reaction by the Club to the Soviet Trials of 1937, in *Soviet Justice and the Trial of Radek* by Dudley Collard; while J. R. Campbell explained the Trotskyite purges in his *Soviet Policy and its Critics*. The total picture, especially of the trials, given in these books, was frankly misleading. It must be admitted, however, that while many people were seriously disturbed by Soviet methods at the time, they temporarily suppressed their doubts in the interests of unity of the Left against the Nazi danger.

As far as the positive achievements of Soviet Russia were concerned a very powerful addition to the arguments and facts of the books was, of course, to go and see for oneself. In conjunction with Prospect Tours, the Club organised a number of specialist tours to the Soviet Union for the purpose of studying Soviet Education, Soviet Medicine and the Agricultural situation. These ended in 1938 owing to the refusal of nearly all the applications for visas, with the growth of international tension.

It was no doubt the belief that "a new civilisation" on the socialist model was coming into existence in Russia which gave persuasiveness and conviction to the Marxist theories of Strachey and others. And when it came to the situation in Western Europe it was they who seemed to have real understanding of the political situation, and were able to make sense of the tangled

[4] The other books must be briefly noted. Hilary Newitt, *The Position of Women in the U.S.S.R.*, Pat Sloan's *Soviet Democracy*, Page Arnot's two-volume *Short History of the Russian Revolution* (in the Educational Series), and two fascinating studies of the Soviet Arctic, Ruth Gruber's *I Went to the Soviet Arctic* and L. Brontman's *On Top of the World*. *Comrades and Citizens,* was a charming and most human account of ordinary people in their homes and at work in Russia as it then was.

international scene. As a consequence their intellectual power and persuasive eloquence, as well as their books which were immensely popular, captured the heart and mind of the Club to an extraordinary degree.

As late as October 1938, that is to say after Munich, we find Gollancz saying, "during the period that the Club has been in existence, the Communist Party has shown complete understanding of the fascist and particularly of the Hitler menace, and superb energy in its attempts to awaken the public to their peril."

The shock of the Munich crisis compelled V.G. to re-examine the whole attitude of the Club to the struggle against fascism. Was it not in some cases becoming propagandist in spirit, not allowing a glimmer of justice to the other side? "With such methods we can have nothing whatever to do,"[5] he said. Was the Club not concentrating "to too great a degree on two or three points of view?" Was it not forgetting that "the whole conception of the Club is that it should produce (politically) a highly educated corps of men and women, prepared to dedicate themselves to the work of spreading the knowledge that they have acquired and of awakening the political consciousness of the indifferent and apathetic."[6] Above all the Club must make one of its main tasks "to be a bulwark of truth and scrupulousness and respect for other people's opinions, and of the most complete freedom of thought and discussion."[7] Finally, we must at all costs avoid falling into the very evils we are combatting, compromising our own values with such notions as "the end justifies the means."

There was no doubt that this pointed to uneasiness as to the Club's uncritical acceptance of communist ideas, and an enthusiasm for Russian achievement insufficiently tempered by a critical attitude to the methods of the Soviet regime.

But after the Soviet-German Pact of non-aggression a revulsion of feeling changed the attitude of very many Club members both to Russia and to communism. But it is necessary to an understanding of the pros and cons of the issue to understand the importance of Hitler's long-term plans for the invasion of Russia, and the counter-measures against German aggression

[5] "Thoughts after Munich" (*Left News,* November 1938).
[6] *Ibid.*
[7] *Ibid.*

which many political groupings had been urging during these momentous years.

The Left Book Club was only one section of the informed opinion which had urgently pressed for a military alliance with Russia as the only possible deterrent to Hitler. The existence of a group energetically working behind the scenes which included Lord Cecil, Duncan Sandys, Wilson Harris of the *Spectator,* Dingle Foot, Sir Arthur Salter and a number of Conservatives, and the Liberals, Sir Archibald Sinclair, Professor Gilbert Murray and Sir Walter Layton, made it clear that there was a considerable body of opinion which held that both our safety and that of Russia was dependent upon the participation of Russia in a firm declaration of military action against further aggression.

It was generally felt that the immediate blow which was expected would be against Poland and Russia. It was thought by some that there were elements in the Government which would not be too concerned if the conflict broke out in the East leaving Western Europe secure. Hence the consternation in these circles when on the failure of her efforts to secure an alliance with Britain and France, Russia staved off immediate danger by her totally unexpected pact of non-aggression with Germany.

The recent publication of still later Cabinet Papers (for 1939) makes it perfectly clear that the Government never had any intention of securing the help of Russia in the event of war.

> The Cabinet Papers for 1939 prove now conclusively that Britain could have had an acceptable alliance with Russia if only Chamberlain and his Ministers had wanted one. Russia needed the alliance and wanted it. Britain needed it but did not want it. Britain, Russia, Poland and France together would almost certainly have deterred Hitler in 1939. The British Government's problem in that year was to find a strong ally in Eastern Europe. It was a problem that Chamberlain and Halifax did not want to face. So they evaded it. In the end the Russians lost patience, and concluded a non-aggression pact with Hitler. . . . During the critical months that followed the dismemberment of Czechoslovakia the Russians appreciated correctly what had to be done to stop Hitler, and Chamberlain did not.[8]

However to very many, and among them Victor Gollancz

[8] The *Guardian* (January 1st, 1970).

and a large part of the Club membership, the Pact appeared to be an act of shameful perfidy, a base betrayal of socialist principles. To make an agreement, an *alliance,* as it seemed, with the worst enemy of all progressive causes and of democracy, appeared to be a shocking example of the doctrine that the end justifies the means even if that end was the preservation of Russia from invasion and the destruction of socialism.

The suppressed doubts and hesitations which V.G. had felt during the past three years now came to the surface. He felt that he had too easily concurred in what from the first he ought to have questioned. The Pact made all this crudely plain, and there could be no more compromise.

The Russo-German Pact thus became the turning point in the development of the Club's thought and policies. It was in fact the beginning of the end.

CHAPTER XI

WHEN WAR CAME

WHEN WAR WAS declared, the first reaction was that the Club must now face a drastic reappraisal of its function, since it could no longer regard the prevention of war as its primary aim. "It is clear," wrote V.G., in the *Left News* for 1939, "that we have the gravest difficulties to face . . . [and that] the duty of all members in their various ways is to do all in their power to win the war and defeat Fascism." Perhaps the biggest contribution the Club could make, he said, would be to keep alive and unimpaired the idea of freedom, and to carry on its basic aim of education in order to secure "greater political consciousness, better political judgment, and more political enthusiasm on the part of our members."

No-one realised at that moment that "the gravest difficulties" were to be the opposition to the war on the part of the Communist Party, and of John Strachey and many Club members, on the one hand, and the reaction of the Club to a drastic change of attitude to Soviet Russia stemming from V.G.'s resolve to free the Club from its one-sided attitude to communism.

With the outbreak of war there was at first unanimity, but when the Communist Party declared a few months later that it was an imperialist war and that they would not support it, for the first time in its history the Club had a divided leadership.

It is not easy to understand the reason for this sudden change. Harry Pollitt had produced a pamphlet entitled *How to Win the War,* and the Central Committee of the Communist Party had issued a manifesto pledging "support of all necessary means to secure the victory of democracy over fascism". But there was at the same time deep suspicion of the motives of the Government. Could Chamberlain really be trusted to lead a war against Germany which he had supported in so many ways for so many years?

Meanwhile nothing much happened in the West for some

months. It was the period of the "phoney war". Leading political
figures, including Lloyd George, were searching for some path
towards the opening of negotiations before it was too late; and,
if it were possible, to enlist Russia in such a venture. This was
also the policy of the Communist Party.

The division of opinion in the leadership of the Club now
emerged in the *Left News*. In the issue for December 1939,
Strachey had an article against the War, and Laski defended it.
Strachey argued that :

> the victory of the Chamberlain and Daladier Governments could
> not possibly result in the war aims of Labour being achieved.
> To propose these aims while supporting the war would only help
> Chamberlain and Daladier to delude their people into fighting
> for wholly reactionary aims.
>
> The way out lies through the struggle of the people of Britain,
> France and Germany, and of every other imperialist power
> against their own governments. We can help to free the Czech
> people by our struggle against our own government.

Strachey concluded that we must therefore demand that the
war be stopped and a world settlement reached.

Laski replied that on the contrary the shortest way to end the
war was for the U.S.S.R. to put the whole of its immense
authority behind the kind of peace that the Labour Party had
declared for, and make it plain to Berlin that it was behind that
policy. Meanwhile no socialist should come down on the side
of peace on any other terms—that would be a betrayal as great
as that of Munich. "Nothing would do so much to heal the
divisions in the ranks of Labour as the knowledge that no
communist, either, was so prepared."

There was a flood of letters in the *Left News,* some denouncing
the Club for not taking sides, and others declaring that in
supporting the war the Club had betrayed socialism. In a long
article in the January issue Gollancz endeavoured to clarify
the position of the Club and indicate the lines of its future
development.

In the first place, he insisted on the freedom of the selectors
and the members to make up their own minds, whether they
decided for the war and against the policy of Russia and of the
Communist Party, or against the war. In future there was to

be *no Club line* on these controversial questions, but open debate.

For several months the debate continued. It became clear that in future the Club was going to pursue a very different course from that of the previous four years. It was now to be an open forum. There was to be no slurring over of differences and conflicting policies, but free and open discussion. *And the same policy would hold with regard to the choice of books.*

> I think it right to add [wrote V.G.] that in my view the publications of the Club have tended to concentrate to too great a degree (though by no means exclusively) on two or three points of view, and to forget that any author has a place in our ranks, provided only that his work is of value in the struggle for peace and a better social and economic order, and against fascism.[1]

From now on, as we shall see, the publications of the Left Book Club were extremely varied both in subject and in political orientation; and the *Left News* instead of pursuing a consistent policy became indeed an open forum for ideas of the widest scope and of greatly differing points of view.

The next shock for the Club came with the publication, in November 1939, of *Barbarians at the Gate* by Leonard Woolf; which was to be followed by the Dean of Canterbury's *Socialist Sixth of the World,* in December.

The author of *Barbarians at the Gate,* Leonard Woolf, was a socialist of long standing with strong liberal principles. He detested fascism, but also saw in Russian politics much that he regarded as totalitarian and immoral. The book, while exposing the barbarism of Germany and Italy, directed the attention of the Club to "the other barbarians". While the fascists alone had openly and brazenly repudiated the standards of European civilisation, and were indeed "Barbarians at the Gate"; yet we too had *all* betrayed those standards: Liberal democrats by refusing to face the necessity for socialism; communists by accepting the position that socialism cannot be established without replacing democratic institutions by the dictatorship of the proletariat. Woolf proceeded to develop this into a sustained polemic against the theory and practice of the Soviet Government.

[1] *Left News* (January 1940).

Strachey was unwilling to agree to its publication unless the selectors allowed him to publish in the *Left News* for that month a critical review of the book. Hence for the first time, a Club choice was opposed by one of the selectors. In his review Strachey complained that Woolf never gave his reasons for rejecting the view that a working class dictatorship is indispensable to the establishment and maintenance of a socialist regime, until the resistance of the exploiting classes is finally crushed. This, argued Strachey, is all that "the dictatorship of the proletariat" means.

Laski replied that Strachey did not tell us how long that dictatorship would have to last or why it seemed to be not so much the dictatorship of the people over a reactionary minority as the dictatorship of the Party over the people. Nor did Strachey seriously consider the problem of getting rid of the apparatus and habits of tyrannical rule.

Woolf's book shocked a large number of members and startled everyone. It indicated a reversal of Club policy of great significance. In future the Club did not stand for *one* faith. It was now prepared to publish books critical of Marxism and to encourage within the Club a variety of conflicting opinions.

It would be a mistake to think that the Club's attitude to Russia had always been a naïve acceptance that all our hopes for a better world had been vindicated. Those who looked hopefully towards the changes going on in Soviet Russia were aware of the circumstances under which the building of socialism was proceeding. After centuries of Czarist autocracy they were not expecting it to be possible to follow the course that some thought might be possible in Britain.

But the exclusion of any possibility of a return to capitalism was seen as the necessary condition of a whole series of liberties not obtainable otherwise : freedom from unemployment, freedom to make the fullest use of the country's resources, a great extension of classless education and so forth. Many therefore believed that some force and some dictatorial measures were inevitable if socialism were to be established in a country like Russia. Some deprecated harsh measures but recognised the enormous achievements, others ignored and excused or explained them away. Even the most critical sadly confessed that after all evils and repression had characterised our own revolution in 1640, the American Revolution in 1776, and the French Revolution in 1789, in fact every great advance in the chequered story of man : "The Web of History is not woven with innocent hands".

But Russia had been of profound significance as far as the prevention of war was concerned. The more the menace of fascism grew, the more we looked to a military alliance with Russia as the only way to prevent war. The more the fascist threat grew the more many Club members saw in Soviet Communism the alternative to fascist reaction. In such circumstances it had been understandable that allowances were made for the short-comings and harshness of the regime.

The controversy about these two events, the opposition to the war on the part of the Communist Party and John Strachey, and the publication of *Barbarians at the Gate,* continued throughout the war, though after a few months Strachey reversed his attitude and again supported the war. Victor Gollancz contributed to the discussion in the *Left News* and by the publication of two books. The first was *The Betrayal of the Left,* the Additional book for February 1941. Edited by Victor Gollancz, its contributors were John Strachey, George Orwell, Professor Laski, and V.G. himself.

More clearly than anything previously published by the Club, this book defined the position of Victor Gollancz himself from this time forward, and marked the end of communist influence in the direction of the Left Book Club. Much of the material was reprinted from the *Left News*. The main theme was a trenchant attack on the decision of the Communist Party not to take up arms against Nazi Germany, which was interpreted as "revolutionary defeatism"—the strategy of working for the overthrow of capitalist imperialism in Britain as the prelude to socialist revolution. This had been Lenin's policy in Russia in 1917, but it may be questioned whether any British communist in 1941 took this line, however misguided their judgment that the war was an "imperialist" one.

One of the most interesting and important sections of the book was the long epilogue on the question of political morality, which was afterwards debated at length in a series of articles and letters in the *Left News* through 1941.

Before the Club came to its end Gollancz published *Our Threatened Values* which was the Club Choice for July 1946. In it V.G. reaffirmed his faith in the ideals of socialism, and also his belief in the immense possibilities which the Russian Revolution had opened for the world. But he went on to say that the totalitarian political control that went with it was wholly evil: "If totalitarianism conquers, and whether it embodies a socialist element or not, the Russian Revolution will turn out to have been of disastrous evil."

CHAPTER XII

THE LAST DAYS OF THE CLUB

THE DECLARATION OF war sealed the fate of the Left Book Club. Its days were numbered. This was not realised at first; but very rapidly a critical situation developed and could not be resolved. The *first* aim of the Club had been "the prevention of war". That is to say, the prevention of a fascist war of aggression. But this could only have been achieved by collective security, and that meant in every democratic country not only the union of the anti-fascist parties in a Popular Front, though that was essential, but that having done so they would unite with other similarly orientated countries in an alliance for the restraint of the Nazi power.

The Popular Front was never achieved in Britain and had been overthrown in France. Collective security had been abandoned and Chamberlain had secured the all but unanimous consent of Parliament for his policy of appeasement.[1]

The Club had failed. In the November (1939) *Left News,* V.G. wrote:

> If we had had half a million members the Government would have been replaced by a People's Government long before the war came and the Anglo-Soviet alliance would have been consummated. Hitler would have been overthrown . . . and the war would never have happened.

But in this we had not succeeded.

All the causes for which we had fought: Spain, Czechoslovakia, Peace, had been defeated.

Now our task was to stand for the democratic values for which we were fighting; to discuss the causes of war and the conditions

[1] The single dissident in the House of Commons was William Gallacher, the Communist Member.

of a permanent peace; to consider the various proposals for a better social order.

The Club had flourished and grown on a fighting policy of *commitment* to basic issues on which we were all united—but now issues had emerged on which we were fundamentally divided. Indeed on the vital issue of Russia it was now doubtful whether it would be possible for those who believed whole-heartedly in the Soviet Union to continue in the same organisation with those who were now profoundly critical of its methods and its basic philosophy.

But the radical opposition which thus appeared did not always divide the members of the groups as drastically as the correspondence columns of the *Left News* suggested might be the case. *Individuals* often felt deeply, and it was they who wrote in to the *Left News*. The members in general were confused, uncertain; *inclined* perhaps to one side or the other, but ready to listen to both sides. What disturbed them was the sudden absence of any lead from V.G. or the selectors. Only gradually did they realise that the Club had ceased to have a policy; that the old confident drive for passionately accepted aims had gone for good and all.

But the groups already had elaborate programmes of lectures, discussions, schools, filmshows, plays and so on; and for months they went on very much as before. The books were still coming out, and were not all of them on the war. (Max Werner's *Military Strength of the Powers* could be discussed usefully whichever side one was on.) Therefore, the "war or no-war" debate could become secondary to the regular programme.

Then the call-up, the direction of labour, the black-out, began to cut down attendance and in the last contribution I made to the *Left News* as Group Organiser I find that I was referring to the fact that "many groups found it extremely difficult to adjust themselves to the completely new situation brought about by the war." I recorded that groups were going out of existence because of timidity, loss of confidence and pessimism : or because they came to consist of members who all believed alike because those who didn't agree had left, and those remaining got bored by never hearing a fresh opinion.

But many of the Left Book Club Groups flourished until the end of the war and after. One of the most important of these was the Hampstead Left Book Club, which with a variety of outside speakers and a vigorous progressive policy was very successful. The Leeds Forum, with its excellent premises, continued to do good work for many years. The groups in Birmingham, Manchester, Accrington, Chesterfield, Rossendale, Stockport and several other towns maintained discussions on contemporary issues.

With the outbreak of war, Gollancz moved a skeleton staff to Brimpton (his country house) and the rest found other work. The Groups Department at Henrietta Street also was closed down and the four field organisers and the Theatre Guild staff, together with the office workers, found themselves looking for jobs. Betty Reid and I continued for some months to give what help we could to the groups; and V.G. came up from the country from time to time. Clearly the day-to-day work could not be carried on as before. All we could do was to keep things ticking over and answer queries from anxious conveners. As the breach widened among the leading members of the groups, if not among the majority, and groups began to pass resolutions and level reproaches at the leadership, it became clear that V.G. could no longer rely on their pursuing the policy he had decided upon—the balanced study of the books, avoidance of settled policies or conclusions, and independence of any one political line. In the summer of 1940 the Groups Department was transferred to Brimpton.

Very shortly afterwards I found myself appointed Staff Lecturer to His Majesty's Forces and busily engaged in lecturing to Army and Air Force units all over Southern England on "The Rise of Fascism", "Nazi Germany", "Europe between Two Wars", then after June 1941, on the U.S.S.R.; and finally on the strategy of the war. By 1944 the Army Bureau of Current Affairs was wisely giving its attention to Britain after the war— to questions of social security, health, housing and education, working with an excellent series of booklets, *British Way and Purpose*. I mention this because my equipment for the job largely consisted of the books issued by the Club. I found that the keen Education Officers were often former Left Book Club members and from time to time men in uniform would come and speak to me after a lecture to announce themselves as members of one of the groups or former members of the Left Book Club. Where there was a permanent military base, as in Egypt, old conveners and members got busy organising political discussion groups and even "parliaments", all of a decidedly *left* complexion.

Perhaps the Club had something to do with the Left opinion which prevailed in the forces towards the end of the war and revealed itself after demobilisation, and also with similar sentiments among civilians, and thus played a part in creating the landslide which brought the Labour Government to power in 1945.

V.G. once described the Club as "The most successful political adventure of our generation" (*Left News,* October 1938). He could say this even in the bitter moment of the Munich betrayal. He added : "And why? Because people *want* to know; because people, when they once learn the truth, have a burning desire to open the eyes of those who have also been blind."

Undoubtedly the series of polemical tracts which Gollancz brought out before the General Election of 1945, small cloth-bound booklets in the familiar yellow dust covers, were enormously influential.

Guilty Men, an indictment of the politicians responsible for Munich, by Cato (Frank Owen, Michael Foot and Peter Howard) was the most trenchant; there followed *Why not Trust the Tories?* by Celticus (Aneurin Bevan, M.P.), and *Can the Tories Win the Peace?* by Diplomaticus (K. Zilliacus).

These found eager readers among the general public but especially among the Club members.

From the outbreak of war until May 1940, V.G. tried to preserve a fair balance between conflicting views about the war both in the *Left News,* in which a fierce controversy raged in the form of articles from one side and the other and a considerable correspondence, and in the books. "Thus we were able to publish Woolf and Cole and Rader as well as Dutt and Hannington and the Dean."[2] During the whole period, V.G. preserved a strict neutrality as editor and made no appeal to the members. The military situation had now become one of grave peril, V.G. wrote an appeal to "Members of the Left Book Club" as an inset to the May issue of the *Left News,* "In the name of Socialism, in the name of every decent and gentle and beloved thing, in the name above all of Freedom", to unite to defend civilisation. The task of the Club was now "to work

[2] Inset to the *Left News* (May 1940).

for the defeat of Hitler", and "to explain everywhere *the necessity of Socialism*" (our italics). It is to be noted that up to the outbreak of war while *in fact* the Club was preaching socialism, it welcomed non-socialists as members, and in its aims of membership spoke only of "a better social and economic order."

In November 1940, V.G. suggested changing the name of the Club to "The League of Victory and Progress". But this was not welcomed and the idea was dropped. He was able to record the overwhelming support of the membership for his appeal in May, and thus the unity of the Club was restored on this basis. In the same issue of the *Left News* V.G. promised that in the months to come he intended to print "highly provocative and controversial articles" on all issues except the question of the war. On that basis the Club was now united.

During these months Strachey was re-examining his position. After Hitler's invasion of the Low Countries he became convinced that the major aspect of the war was indeed the defence of western civilisation. He now rejoined Gollancz and Laski, returned to the Labour Party, and served as Parliamentary Under-Secretary of State, Minister of Food, and Secretary of State for War in Attlee's post-war Labour Government. His review of the whole situation, and of the economic perspective as he now saw it, appeared in the *Left News* for May 1942.

In February 1941, V.G. could announce that "the Club's life is quickening". In his advertisements he was now saying

WIN THE WAR : and WIN IT BY AND FOR SOCIALISM

In April came a new statement as "What the Club *is*" :

> We see the Club as a body of politically educated men and women who regard it as their function to think out honestly and clearly the problems that confront us.

This was to mean the conversion of the masses to socialism by the widespread distribution of books, *but also* by an appeal not only to reason but to idealism, and not only to the workers but to the middle class, the technicians, the salariat (*Left News*, April 1941).

New writers now began to appear in the *Left News*. George Orwell wrote a series of articles on the theme that "Either we turn England into a socialist democracy or by one route or

another we become part of the Nazi empire : there is no third
alternative." (*Left News*, January 1941.) Sir Richard Acland,
who was now starting his new organisation for the common
ownership of land and industry—"The Forward March", began
to insist strongly on the necessity for the higher ethical appeal
in the fight for socialism, and to oppose Strachey's now emphatic
claims for a mixed economy, part capitalist, part socialist; his
emphasis being on democratically controlled capitalism as the
next step towards socialism. The class struggle, he declared,
is about "who is to use the central control."

In May 1942, Gollancz called the *War-time Conference* of
the Club. This met on May 30th and 31st at the Royal Hotel,
London, and was well attended. The Christian Left was represented by the Bishop of Bradford who spoke at some length.
The proceedings developed into a debate between Sir Richard
Acland and Professor Laski : Acland advocating a new socialist
society standing for common ownership and with a strong ethical
impulse, Laski for reinvigorating and then supporting the Labour
Party.

Meanwhile the new policy as to the books was coming into
effect. The Club now had books of a socialist or even an
unorthodox Marxist character which would not have appeared
when the Communist influence on the Club was strong.

In April 1940 came Frölich's *Rosa Luxemburg: Her Life and
Work*. In November of the same year came Lucien Laurat's
Marxism and Democracy. Rosa Luxemburg was a Marxist of
great influence, who was murdered by the police in the German
Revolution of 1918. Perhaps second only to Lenin in the years
of the First World War, she disagreed with him in expecting
the whole working class to move forward to socialism at that
time, and was highly critical of Lenin's party and its policies.
Lucien Laurat, also took a Marxist point of view that was
strongly opposed to that of the Russian Communist Party,
rejecting the Soviet claim to have achieved a classless society and
affirming that capitalist economic development had reached a
higher standard, even though it should now be controlled democratically, that is to say become socialised.

In August 1940 Leo Huberman, whose book *Man's Worldly
Goods* had been a popular choice, wrote *We, the People,* a
brilliant and captivating history of the United States from the
War of Independence to the present day, with a sketch of its

origins. A defence of French democracy came from the pen of Louis Lévy in *France is a Democracy* (August 1943), and then two more excellent books on Germany, Franz Neumann's *Behemoth: The Structure and Practice of National Socialism* (which was probably a better book than the original Club choice by Brady, *The Spirit and Structure of German Fascism*); A. Ramos Oliveira's *A People's History of Germany* appeared in April 1942.

In April 1939 Max Werner's *The Military Strength of the Powers* had been published, rejecting the view that Russia's military capacity was negligible. Events proved the correctness of Werner's judgment, even though her strength had been weakened by the purges of officers, and not correctly deployed in June 1941 because of Stalin's credulous trust in Hitler. Werner issued two other books, *Battle for the World: The Strategy and Diplomacy of the Second World War* (June 1941), and *The Great Offensive: The Strategy of Coalition Warfare* (January 1943). If the Club had not been so preoccupied with its internal troubles these books would have proved profoundly encouraging.

Sir John Maynard's *The Russian Peasant and Other Studies* (September and October, 1942), was a first hand account of internal conditions in Russia before the war with important chapters from an impartial point of view on Soviet policy, religion and the possibility of the development of personality out of collectivism.

New light was thrown on the diplomatic moves in Berlin leading up to the War by the American Ambassador's reminiscences. *Ambassador Dodd's Diary* became the Additional book for March 1941. It cast a flood of light into the dark passages of the time when Hitler was solidifying and expanding his dominion in Germany. It is likely to be regarded for years to come as a priceless source of primary information as well as an intriguing human document.

From the early days of the Club non-members could obtain a six-month subscription to the *Left News* for 2s. 6d.[3] It had always been far more than the Club news-sheet. Its lengthy topical articles and full-scale reviews, its policy of publishing important documents and speeches made it valuable in itself as well as the organ of Club policy. As the Club grew, it auto-

[3] Subsequently raised to 3s.

matically gained the largest circulation of any political journal in Britain.

When war was declared, for several months it was devoted to vigorous controversy in the form of articles, critical replies, and correspondence. It then began to assume a new form. The Club, for the first month after the declaration of war, had no programme and the books reflected a variety of opinions. The *Left News* now became the vehicle for the full and vigorous expression of considered opinion and serious debate by people of different opinions.

Eventually while some books again aroused great interest, many of them made little impression, and the *Left News* itself increased in importance, and later perhaps became even more important than the books. With the incorporation of *The International Socialist Forum,* which will be mentioned shortly, it must have been read by more and more non-members. Club news disappeared and later not even the Club choices were announced. The last reference to the Choice of the Month appeared in December 1944. The *Left News* itself ceased publication in March 1947. The Club came to an end in October 1948.

Three important developments in the *Left News* during 1941 were, first, the welcome given by Gollancz to the Christian Left. Regular articles began to appear by Sidney Dark, the editor of the *Church Times,* Kenneth Ingram, and the Rev. L. J. Collins, later Canon Collins and a close associate and friend of V.G. in later days. Contributions from the Christian Left now became a regular feature of the *Left News*. Also from the Christian point of view came a full length article, scholarly and fair minded but strongly critical, by Professor H. G. Wood on "Christianity and Marxist Philosophy" (*Left News,* August 1943). Secondly a series of discussion articles on "Ethics" was published consisting of contributions from Acland, Strachey, Olaf Stapledon, and others. A vigorous correspondence followed, revealing profound disagreements. One of the best contributions came from Professor John Macmurray.

The third innovation was the monthly twelve-page Supplement, *International Socialist Forum,* edited by the Austrian socialist Julius Braunthal. This represented the views of the left-wing socialist colony of émigrés from Western Europe, and until the *Left News* ceased publication they carried on a vigorous and well informed discussion on the future of Europe after the war.

G. D. H. Cole raised the question of the post-war balance of power in Europe in an article in the *Left News* for August 1941. He wrote under the pseudonym of "Populus" and his ideas were subsequently elaborated in his book *Europe, Russia and the Future* (the choice for October 1941). In his article he said that after the war

> it may be that the government of continental Europe will be divided between the two great States—an enlarged Soviet Union in the east and south, and a new West European State, embracing the countries which have a more deeply rooted liberal tradition.

In subsequent issues this was strongly criticised by some and defended by others. In the event it was Cole's prediction that came nearest to fulfilment.

Cole also started a vigorous discussion on the Future of Trade Unionism, opposing the Labour view of Herbert Tracey, who could see no farther than the continuance of Trade Union efforts to secure the best conditions possible under capitalism. Cole argued for the socialist control of industry itself.

As the war developed and drew towards its end, the German question came to the fore. V.G. strongly opposed Vansittart's bitter condemnation of all Germans, and began to fight for a more charitable attitude to the enemy. In the same spirit and following the strong ethical lead of earlier discussions he pleaded for a return to the spirit of early socialism, its idealism and spiritual fervour, and lamented the loss of the evangelical spirit. V.G. strongly disagreed with Strachey who rejected all absolute ethical principles and insisted on the complete relativism of ethical judgments, as did many other Marxists.

In 1942 the *Left News* began to serialise books already published or to be published separately. The first of these was Ruth Benedict's *Race and Racism* (a Routledge publication). Another book to be serialised was Strachey's original pamphlet *Why You Should be a Socialist,* and Gollancz's own book, *Shall Our Children Live or Die? A Reply to Lord Vansittart on the German Problem* appeared in this form. The *Left News* also published a number of verbatim reports of the Parliamentary proceedings when important discussions took place on the issues which were being dealt with from month to month in the journal.

There was a sudden return of interest in 1945 following the Labour Victory in the General Election. V.G.'s Editorials had not appeared since August 1941, though occasionally there were brief Announcements. Now once more, in August 1945, Victor Gollancz gave us a very typical example. It was entitled *The Left Book Club and The Labour Victory*. It was in fact a Retrospect, a brief review of the whole story of the Club.

It concluded by reminding us that the following friends, members of and speakers for the Club were now members of His Majesty's Government: The Prime Minister, Sir Stafford Cripps, Ellen Wilkinson, Aneurin Bevan, Emanuel Shinwell, Philip Noel-Baker, Lord Addison, John Strachey; and the following have just been elected Members of Parliament: Maurice Edelman, Michael Foot, Elwyn Jones, J. P. W. Mallalieu, Stephen Swingler and K. Zilliacus. V.G. ended by promising a further article on "the supreme opportunity—and obligation— which now awaits us", but this never appeared.

It remains to mention one or two exceptionally interesting books issued by the Club in the war years. Professor Laski only wrote one book for the Club. It was his *Faith, Reason and Civilisation,* a search for the source of new values, and a criticism of some of the irrational ideologies that bedevilled the pre-war years and did much to undermine rational faith in man and his future. V.G. himself wrote two books passionately concerned with the divided counsels of the Club. The first was *The Betrayal of the Left* and its contents have been sufficiently indicated; the second, published as the choice for July 1946 was *Our Threatened Values*. Stating that the one supreme value was the sacredness of personality, and then that the pursuit of this or any other value never, under any circumstances, justified the use of means other than those which are good in themselves, V.G. vigorously criticised all forms of dictatorship as destructive of personality, and all means to achieve social ends which involved "the suppression of the true and the suggestions of the false", or which "treat men not as ends in themselves, but as means to an outside end." The second half of the book criticised the Potsdam Agreement, the treatment of Germany after the war, and the whole post-war international policy of the Allies from the standpoint of the moral ideals he so passionately believed in and advocated.

The last book issued by the Club was G. D. H. Cole's *The Meaning of Marxism*. It was a revised version of his earlier book, *What Marx Really Meant,* published in 1934. If this book (in either version) had been widely read by the Club members a good deal of the dogmatic Marxism, of later versions than Marx's own, might have been less acceptable, and the Club's conceptions of Marxist theory would have been less open to criticism. Cole wrote more books for the Club than any other author—eight in all—Strachey wrote seven.

By 1948 the Club membership, after a sharp drop in 1939 followed by a period of recovery, had declined. Between 1939 and 1942 it fell from 57,000 to 15,000, then finally to 7,000. With the issue of the last choice, *The Meaning of Marxism*, in November 1948, Victor Gollancz announced his decision that the Left Book Club should now cease. He wrote in the last issue of the *Left News* :

> In view of a totally changed situation, we have been feeling for some time that there is a certain artificiality about the continuation of the Club. Political education and, in particular, the education of the electorate in the principles of socialism are more vitally important than ever but we feel that this work can now best be carried on not on a membership basis but by providing, at the cheapest possible price, suitable books for mass circulation to the general public.

*   *   *

As I look back on this story of most varied activity in which so many famous names appear, one recalls how natural it was for writers and musicians, actors and poets, scientists and doctors to feel that they belonged to, and were proud to be associated with the Club.

At this time the tide of intelligent opinion was running our way, and the Club for its part was helping to make it run, and expressing with a certain amount of clarity the aspirations, the indignations, the questioning, and above all the convictions of those days. We were the voice of the times, as far as the fear of, and the anger at, fascism was concerned, as far as the passionate desire for peace and a more humane future for society was concerned. So many people really cared, really tried to face their responsibilities in these critical years.

Then the tide turned. There came the shock of the confusing days before the war; the shame of Munich, the failure to compel the Government to form an effective united front with Russia. Then came the Soviet-German Pact, which really marked the end of an era. All these contributed to the uncertainty and confusion of these months, and to the appearance of divided opinions.

The faith of many inside and outside the Club faded. Members and former friends found themselves in different camps, or once more isolated from the welter of conflicting tendencies. The unity of the Club had gone. It lost its momentum. We went our different ways.

APPENDIX I

THE MEN WHO MADE THE CLUB

John Strachey

John Strachey, the son of the former editor of the *Spectator* in its great days, was educated at Eton and Magdalen, Oxford. He came to notice in the twenties as the young Labour M.P. for Aston, where he later became the ally of Sir Oswald Mosley, the Labour Candidate for the Ladywood Division. Together they produced an ingenious remedy for unemployment based on rather questionable monetary theories. He became a member of Mosley's New Party, but withdrew when the real nature of Mosley's movement became apparent.

Strachey had the scholar's passion for understanding things, and an open-minded concern for new ideas. When the economic crisis appeared in 1929 he accepted the Marxist diagnosis of the situation. He saw no possibility of the capitalist class yielding to the demand for social change that seemed to it destructive of its interests. But even before the outbreak of the Second World War the influence of Keynes and Roosevelt's New Deal suggested an alternative to revolution, while a new flexibility in the political attitude of capitalist governments appeared in their alliance with Russia against the fascist dictatorships. Eventually as he explained in his "Political Letter" to the Club in the *Left News* for May 1941 :

> The twenty years' experience of my political life finally convinced me that it is indispensable to take a different road. It is indispensable to put less strain on people. For we know that they simply will not take the strain of being asked to follow the communist path; for it is not the case that no other path is open to them.

His books began to appear in the thirties and were at once recognised as putting what might be called the Marxist approach in new and convincing terms, devoid of jargon, and extremely lucid. *The Coming Struggle for Power* and *The Meaning of Fascism* seemed to the intelligent man seeking a way through world chaos, to be a completely convincing and exciting explanation of what was happening. Strachey was closely associated for some years with the Communist Party and *The Daily Worker*, for which he wrote regularly, but he never actually joined the Party.

He became, without question, the intellectual force behind the Left Book Club. His books and his articles in the *Left News* provided the Marxist theory behind contemporary problems which the Club assimilated. He was the great *explainer*. He was clear, illuminating, concrete and very persuasive. He lectured and spoke regularly for the Club, and this extended the range and impact of his personality.

He was constantly in and out of Henrietta Street and discussed with V.G. almost every book that was issued and every turn of policy of the Club.

Towards the end his socialism became more and more pragmatic and ingenious; less revolutionary and more concerned with the first steps of the transition to socialism which a progressive coalition of Liberals, Labour and Communists might take.

When war came, he first opposed it; then accepted it. He joined the Royal Air Force and did a good deal of broadcasting. In 1945 he joined the Labour Government as Minister of Food and then Minister of Defence. At this time he wrote a new series of books to demonstrate how progressive reforms had outdated Marx's theory of the inevitable worsening of conditions under capitalism. Once again he modified and adapted to cover the requirements of any Labour Government his pragmatic scheme for gradualism, which in his first book, *The Struggle for Power*, he had condemned as likely to prove only "Gradualism in reverse gear." He died unexpectedly in 1963 before he had the chance to convince a perplexed Labour Government of the practicality of his policies. He was a most competent and ingenious theorist, but not too closely acquainted with the trade union movement or the working class. Keith Feiling, his Conservative critic, spoke of "the unbalanced excitement of his bookish mind." Nevertheless, he had the capacity to induce people to think intelligently about political and economic problems which have got to be solved and not shelved. The Club could not have got off the ground without him; but he could not have done nearly so much without the Club.

Harold Laski

Laski was Professor of Political Science at the London School of Economics. He was an able and sympathetic teacher, much loved and appreciated by his students, whatever their political views. He wrote a very great deal, always lucidly and with competent scholarship.

His traditions were Benthamite and Liberal; he was a thinker very much after the pattern of John Stuart Mill. But he came to see the inevitability of socialism as the form of economic organisation appropriate to a developed capitalism. However, he believed that any attempt by constitutional means to change the system would meet with violent opposition from the capitalist class. This he saw as the real meaning of fascism. He thus accepted certain Marxist conceptions which he blended with his Liberal and Labour sympathies.

He was popular in the Labour movement and a brilliant and witty speaker. A member of the Labour Party Executive at one time and then Chairman, he never broke with the Party but angered Transport House with his Marxist views and his association with the Left Book Club.

There were thus certain contradictions in his mind—as there were in all our minds in the thirties. He made these difficulties articulate. He compelled his readers, his students and his hearers to think for themselves. It could well be said of him in Strachey's words in the *Left News*:

> He who supposes that an Englishman of the present day can find his way either to intellectual certainty and political consistency, without doubts, hesitation and errors, shows little appreciation of the gravity or complexity of the present situation.

He brought to the Club, as one of the triumvirate, the authority of his scholarship, the integrity and conviction of his socialism and his loyalty to the Labour movement. He had close acquaintance with American universities, and was as well known in the States as in England; he had many staunch American friends.

He wrote one book for the Club and it was an important one—*Faith, Reason and Civilisation*. These were the three things he lived and worked for.

Beyond his ever ready advice and help on the board of Selectors, he wrote lengthy and critical reviews of many of the books. He died long before his work for scholarship and socialism was completed in 1950.

Victor Gollancz

Only those who knew him and worked with him can appreciate V.G.'s immense capacity for organisation and initiative, his tireless energy and enthusiasm, the competence in the direction of his many enterprises, and his exceptional gift for seizing every opportunity for new ventures.

He placed the resources of his publishing house behind the Club, but any idea that he reaped a rich profit from it is quite false. The advertising was on the largest scale, the Club leaflets were issued by the hundred-thousand. The publishing overheads were enormously increased by the Groups Department with six senior organisers and a full secretarial staff, by the establishment of the department on the whole of the third floor of a central London office block and the very substantial figure for stationery and postage. If the Club ever made money it was after the advertising ceased and the Groups Department was closed down—that is to say after the Club as an organisation based on the groups had come to an end.

V.G. had a fine intellect and a wonderful flair for recognising a good book, or a good man or woman to work in his organisation. His sheer competence and drive, resourcefulness and initiative in seeking out new ventures, allowed him to pursue his plans with incredible efficiency and persistence. Only those who worked closely with him could fully appreciate his exacting attention to detail. He had an alarmingly critical eye for anything that might be neglected or carelessly carried out.

Behind this exactitude V.G. had a great warmth of feeling. He was a deeply emotional man, who put passionate conviction into everything he did. But his evaluation of a person or a policy and his emotional reactions, could change dramatically, and when they did so he could fail to recognise how differently he had been thinking and feeling only a few weeks or months previously.

His personal relations with all who worked for him were close and warm; less perhaps on the business side than in matters concerning the Club itself. He could be generous, overwhelmingly so, but he could be angry and unreasonable, sometimes with insufficient cause. But one could never separate the virtues and the vices of V.G. for the man was a whole person and you took him as you found him or not at all. If you worked for him your affection and loyalty carried you beyond complaining at the violent storms or maddening distortions of feeling and judgement which could sweep over him.

The Club was unthinkable without him; and there was no nonsense about a committee to run the Groups Organisation! He was the directing, inspiring and energising force behind every activity of the Club from the least to the most spectacular. When the end came, a revulsion of feeling paralysed his effort and conviction for a moment. He made one last effort to reinvigorate the Club by changing its whole aim and method; but the divisions within and the shattering blows of the ever-changing war-situation and its international contradictions, were too much for him. When his own passionate faith wavered and his mind shifted its focus, his world changed very rapidly. Suddenly the whole concept and vision of the Club faded. Other causes, other visions supervened. The direction of his mind, his conscience, and his deepest convictions turned elsewhere. The steam went out of the driving energy behind the Club—and that was the end.

What Lord Morley said of Edmund Burke could truly be said of Victor Gollancz :

> He abounded in that active self-confidence and self-assertion which is natural in men who are conscious of great powers and strenuous in promoting great causes.

One of these causes, to which he devoted five crowded years of his life was the Left Book Club.

APPENDIX II

CHRONOLOGICAL LIST OF THE MONTHLY CHOICES AND OTHER SELECTIONS

The first book listed for each month is that month's choice. Optional books are identified in their series as follows: Additional books (A), Supplementary books (S), Topical books (T), Educational series (E), Reprints of Classics (R), and Pamphlets (P). Dual selections are bracketed.

1936	May	FRANCE TODAY AND THE PEOPLE'S FRONT
		Maurice Thorez
		OUT OF THE NIGHT
		H. J. Muller
	June	HITLER THE PAWN
		Rudolf Olden
	July	WORLD POLITICS 1918–1936
		R. Palme Dutt
	August	DAYS OF CONTEMPT
		André Malraux
		CHOOSE A BRIGHT MORNING
		Hillel Bernstein
	September	WALLS HAVE MOUTHS
		Wilfrid Macartney
		POVERTY AND PUBLIC HEALTH (A)
		G. C. M. M'Gonigle and J. Kirby
	October	UNDER THE AXE OF FASCISM
		Gaetano Salvemini

THE PRIVATE MANUFACTURE OF
ARMAMENTS (A)
Philip Noel-Baker

November   THE THEORY AND PRACTICE OF SOCIALISM
John Strachey

THE STRUGGLE FOR PEACE (A)
Stafford Cripps

December   SPAIN IN REVOLT
Harry Gannes and Theodore Repard

AN ATLAS OF CURRENT AFFAIRS (A)
J. F. Horrabin

1937 January   FORWARD FROM LIBERALISM
Stephen Spender

THE POSITION OF WOMEN IN THE
U.S.S.R. (A)
G. N. Serebrennikov

THE NAZI CONSPIRACY IN SPAIN (T)
[Otto Katz]

February   THE PARIS COMMUNE OF 1871
Frank Jellinek

AN ATLAS OF EMPIRE (A)
J. F. Horrabin

RAW MATERIALS OR WAR MATERIALS? (A)
Alfred Plummer

THE PROTECTION OF THE PUBLIC
FROM AERIAL ATTACK (T)
Cambridge Scientists Anti-war Group

March   THE ROAD TO WIGAN PIER
George Orwell

FREUD AND MARX (A)
Reuben Osborn

SOVIET JUSTICE AND THE TRIAL OF
RADEK AND OTHERS (T)
Dudley Collard

DEFENCE OF MADRID (T)
Geoffrey Cox

April   MAN'S WORLDLY GOODS
Leo Huberman

THE CONDITION OF BRITAIN (A)
G. D. H. Cole and M. I. Cole

THE ROAD TO WAR (T)
"Vigilantes" [K. Zilliacus]

May   SOVIET DEMOCRACY
Pat Sloan

A TEXTBOOK OF MARXIST PHILOSOPHY (A)
John Lewis, ed.

CHRISTIANITY AND THE SOCIAL REVOLUTION
(S)
John Lewis; Karl Polanyi; and Donald
K. Kitchen, ed.

THE CITIZEN FACES WAR (S)
Robert Donington and Barbara Donington

THE ROAD TO WIGAN PIER [PART ONE
ONLY] (S)
George Orwell

REPORT OF A RELIGIOUS DELEGATION
TO SPAIN (T)
Hewlett Johnson and Others

June   THE POST-WAR HISTORY OF THE
BRITISH WORKING CLASS
Allen Hutt

HITLER'S CONSPIRACY AGAINST PEACE (A)
S. Erckner

CHANGING MAN : THE EDUCATION
SYSTEM IN THE U.S.S.R. (S)
Beatrice King

WOMEN MUST CHOOSE (S)
Hilary Newitt

WAITING FOR LEFTY (S)
Clifford Odets

SIX MEN OF DORSET (S)
Miles Malleson and H. Brooks

July THE PEOPLE'S FRONT
G. D. H. Cole

TOWARDS THE CHRISTIAN REVOLUTION (A)
R. B. Y. Scott and Gregory Vlastos, ed.

MODERN MARRIAGE AND BIRTH CONTROL (S)
Edward F. Griffith

MOSCOW 1937 (T)
Lion Feuchtwanger

A HANDBOOK OF MARXISM (R)
Emile Burns, ed.

MONEY (E)
Emile Burns

August THE LABOUR PARTY IN PERSPECTIVE
C. R. Attlee

YOUTH IN BRITISH INDUSTRY (A)
John Gollan

FOR PEACE AND FRIENDSHIP (S)
Proceedings of the Second National Congress of Peace and Friendship with the U.S.S.R.

THE TOWN LABOURER, 1760–1832 (R)
J. L. Hammond and Barbara Hammond

THE ACQUISITIVE SOCIETY (R)
R. H. Tawney

AN INTRODUCTION TO PHILOSOPHY (E)
John Lewis

December SPANISH TESTAMENT
Arthur Koestler

LEON BLUM, MAN AND STATESMAN (A)
Geoffrey Fraser and Thadée Natanson

A SHORT HISTORY OF THE RUSSIAN
REVOLUTION, VOL. II (E)
R. Page Arnot

1938 January A PHILOSOPHY FOR A MODERN MAN
H. Levy

LITERATURE AND SOCIETY (A)
David Daiches

RACISM (S)
Magnus Hirshfeld

THE LABOUR SPY RACKET (S)
Leo Huberman

THE LAW OF POLITICAL UNIFORMS, PUBLIC
MEETINGS AND PRIVATE ARMIES (S)
Joseph Baker

WAR CAN BE AVERTED (T)
Eleanor F. Rathbone

AN INTERPRETATION OF BIOLOGY (E)
Henry Collier

February PROMISED LAND
Cedric Belfrage

OUR STREET (S)
Jan Petersen
Neil Hunter

PEASANTRY AND CRISIS IN FRANCE (S)

THE CIVILISATION OF GREECE AND ROME (E)

Benjamin Farrington

March   WHAT ARE WE TO DO?
John Strachey

CAN CAPITALISM LAST? (A)
Frederick Allen

THE LEFT SONG BOOK (S)
Alan Bush and Randall Swingler, ed.

TRADE UNIONISM (E)
John A. Mahon

April   ON TOP OF THE WORLD
L. Brontman

THE PSYCHOLOGY OF REACTION (A)
R. Osborn

CIVIL LIBERTIES (E)
W. H. Thompson

May   A PEOPLE'S HISTORY OF ENGLAND
A. L. Morton

THE JUVENILE LABOUR MARKET (A)
John Jewkes and Sylvia Jewkes

WHY THE LEAGUE HAS FAILED (E)
"Vigilantes" [K. Zilliacus]

WHY YOU SHOULD BE A SOCIALIST (P)
John Strachey

June   AN AMERICAN TESTAMENT
Joseph Freeman

THE CIVIL WAR IN SPAIN (A)
Franz Jellinek

CZECHOSLOVAKIA (S)
Edgar P. Young

SCIENCE AND LIFE (E)
J. G. Crowther

July JUSTICE IN ENGLAND
"A Barrister" [Mavis Hill]

THE WAR AGAINST THE WEST (A)
Aurel Kolnai

WHAT WAR MEANS (T)
H. J. Temperley

ITALIAN FASCISM (E)
Gaetano Salvemini

August THE BATTLE FOR PEACE
F. Elwyn Jones

NINE DAYS THAT SHOOK ENGLAND (A)
H. Fagan

WHY CAPITALISM MEANS WAR (E)
H. N. Brailsford

September A. R. P.
J. B. S. Haldane

THE STRUGGLE FOR RELIGIOUS FREEDOM
IN GERMANY (A)

A. S. Duncan-Jones

A SHORT HISTORY OF THE UNEMPLOYED (E)
Wal Hannington

THE TRUTH ABOUT SPAIN (P)
H. R. G. Greaves and David Thomson

October SECRET AGENT OF JAPAN
Amleto Vespa

EXILES IN THE AEGEAN (A)
Bert Birtles

PEOPLE AT BAY (S)
Oscar I. Janowski

WHY WE ARE LOSING THE PEACE (A)
"Vigilantes" [K. Zilliacus]

THE LEVELLERS AND THE ENGLISH
REVOLUTION (E)

"Henry Holorenshaw" [Joseph
Needham]

ACT NOW : AN APPEAL TO THE MIND
AND HEART OF BRITAIN (P)
Hewlett Johnson

April   THE MILITARY STRENGTH OF THE POWERS
Max Werner

RICHES AND POVERTY (E)
Gordon Schaffer

IS MR. CHAMBERLAIN SAVING PEACE? (P)
Victor Gollancz

May   THE NEW PROPAGANDA
Amber Blanco White

PENN'ORTH OF CHIPS (A)
Charles S. Segal

CHEMISTRY : A SURVEY (E)
Alan Beck

June   THESE POOR HANDS
B. L. Coombes

BLANQUI (A)
Neil Stewart

WHAT IS MARXISM? (E)
Emile Burns

July   TORY M.P.
Simon Haxey

THE CORPORATE STATE IN ACTION (A)
Carl T. Schmidt

	March	TEN LEAN YEARS Wal Hannington
	April	ROSA LUXEMBURG Paul Frölich
	May	INDIA TO-DAY R. Palme Dutt
	June	PRODUCTION FOR THE PEOPLE Frank Verulam
	July	SWASTIKA NIGHT Murray Constantine
	August	WE, THE PEOPLE Leo Huberman
	September	FEDERALISM OR SOCIALISM? John Strachey
	October	LEFT WING DEMOCRACY IN THE ENGLISH CIVIL WAR David W. Petegorsky
	November	MARXISM AND DEMOCRACY Lucien Laurat
	December	FAREWELL, FRANCE! Oscar Paul
1941	January	A FAITH TO FIGHT FOR John Strachey
	February	RATS! "The Pied Piper" [J. P. W. Mallalieu] THE BETRAYAL OF THE LEFT (A) Victor Gollancz, ed.
	March	SCORCHED EARTH, Part I Edgar Snow AMBASSADOR DODD'S DIARY (A) William E. Dodd

April   SCORCHED EARTH, Part 2
Edgar Snow

MY DEAR CHURCHILL (A)
"Populus" [G. D. H. Cole]

May   THE SCUM OF THE EARTH
Arthur Koestler

June   BATTLE FOR THE WORLD
Max Werner

July   THE NAZI NEW ORDER IN POLAND
Jon Evans

August   RUSSIA IN FLUX
John Maynard

September   PRODUCTION FOR VICTORY, NOT PROFIT!
Maurice Edelman

October   EUROPE, RUSSIA AND THE FUTURE
G. D. H. Cole

November   PIERRE LAVAL
Henry Torres

December   WHAT IT WILL BE LIKE IN THE NEW BRITAIN
Richard Acland

1942   January   JAPAN'S KAMPF
Jaya Deva

February   GUILTY GERMANS?
Aubrey Douglas Smith

March   UNDERGROUND EUROPE CALLING
Oscar Paul

April   A PEOPLE'S HISTORY OF GERMANY
A. Ramos Oliveira

May   MISSION TO MOSCOW, Part I
Joseph E. Davies

June   MISSION TO MOSCOW, Part II
            Joseph E. Davies

July   "PASSED TO YOU, PLEASE"
            J. P. W. Mallalieu

August   BEHEMOTH
            Franz Neumann

September   THE RUSSIAN PEASANT : AND OTHER
                              STUDIES, Part I
            John Maynard

October   THE RUSSIAN PEASANT : AND OTHER
                              STUDIES, Part II
            John Maynard

November   GREAT BRITAIN IN THE POST-WAR WORLD
            G. D. H. Cole

December   SOMETHING WENT WRONG
            Lewis Browne

1943 January   THE GREAT OFFENSIVE
                 Max Werner

      February   WILL GERMANY CRACK?
                 Paul Hagen

      March   THE BLACK MAN'S BURDEN
                 John Burger

      April   SUBJECT INDIA
                 H. N. Brailsford

      May   NEED GERMANY SURVIVE?
                 Julius Braunthal

      June   THEY CAME AS FRIENDS
                 Tor Myklebost

      July   APPEASEMENT'S CHILD
                 Thomas J. Hamilton

      August   FRANCE IS A DEMOCRACY
                 Louis Levy

June   THE COMING CRISIS
              Fritz Sternberg

Summer   BEHIND THE SILKEN CURTAIN
              Bartley C. Crum

September   ADVENTURE IN THE SUN
              Maurice Pearlman

October   AUSTRIAN REQUIEM
              Kurt von Schuschnigg

November   WHEN SMUTS GOES
              Arthur M. Keppel-Jones

December   SO MANY HUNGERS
              Bhabani Bhattacharya

1948 January   SOCIALISM OF THE WEST
              Leo Moulin

February   THE CO-OPERATIVE MOVEMENT IN
                                LABOUR BRITAIN
              N. Barou

March   LABOUR, LIFE AND POVERTY
              F. Zweig

April   PRISONERS OF FEAR
              Ella Lingens-Reiner

May   KAFFIRS ARE LIVELY
              Oliver Walker

June   HOW LONG THE NIGHT
              Lina Haag

Summer   THE TRAGEDY OF AUSTRIA
              Julius Braunthal

September   MEN IN THE PITS
              F. Zweig

October   THE MEANING OF MARXISM
              G. D. H. Cole

INDEX